Andrée **Putman**

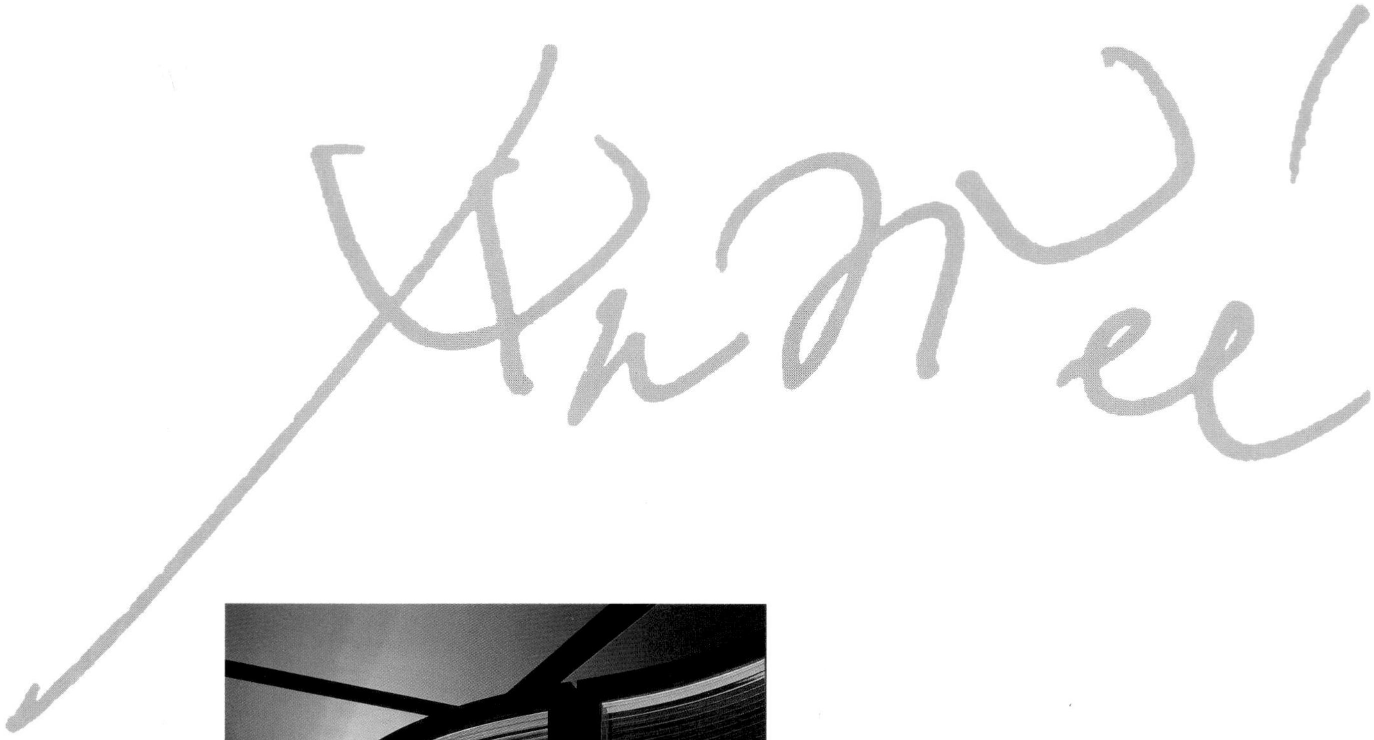

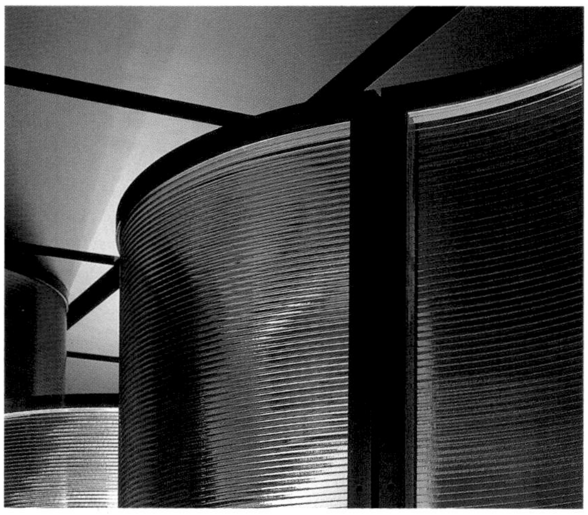

Sophie Tasma-Anargyros

The Overlook Press

Woodstock • New York

First published in 1997 by
The Overlook Press
Lewis Hollow Road
Woodstock, New York 12498

Library of Congress Cataloging-in-Publication Data

Tasma-Anargyros, Sophie
   [Andrée Putman. English]
   Andrée Putman / Sophie Tasma-Anargyros; [translated
from the French].
p. cm.
Includes index.
1. Putman, Andrée—Criticism and interpretation.
2. Interior decoration—
History—20th century. I. Title.
NK2049.Z9P873813 1997 72-.092—dc21   96-45711   CIP
ISBN: 0-87951-936-3
Translated from French by Sue Rose
Designed by Michael Phillips
Printed in Hong Kong
987654321

Acknowledgments

Andrée Putman and Sophie Tasma-Anargyros would like
to extend their very special thanks to: Linda Andrieux, James
Cunningham, Antonio Fournier Condé, Jane Havell, Daniane
Karpus, Sébastien Leclerc, Bruno Moinard, Michael Phillips,
Natacha Portais, Deidi von Schaewen and Francisca Suarez.
Without them, this book would not have been possible.

Contents

Introduction

Andrée Putman loves stories more than anything else in the world, stories with or without words: Sandrine Bonnaire's face in Pialat's film, *A nos amours*, which she has just seen again; the enigma of a canvas, painted by an artist who is possibly unknown, whom she has just discovered; the mysterious wall built in the middle of a field by the hero of a story by Paul Auster; the dialogue in the play *Le temps et la chambre*, directed by Patrice Chéreau, or the compulsive circling of Philip Glass's music. All of these are narratives, told by film, painting, literature, theatre and also - when Bob Wilson's obsessional figures haunt the stage - by dance; by listening carefully, meditatively and sharply, you can discover when it too picks up the thread of the story, conveying the emotion of a final encounter.

But these stories which range through the mind belong to the present; the quest for more is never-ending, as is the quest for new projects, for the meaning of events or any other quest. Andrée Putman is indefatigable; she never stops, and even when she is deliberating, day-dreaming or taking a walk for relaxation, these activities are still an indication that there is a searching sensibility at work.

However, the stories in question are not just those which are narrated by any artistic medium; there are also instantaneous stories, trivial or momentous, which turn up as you round the next bend or which come to the surface when dredged up from the depths of memory by chance. [At Ecart, a young American architect comes into the room and Andrée Putman describes how she bumped into him one morning on the Quai Voltaire. He was a complete stranger and he stopped to tell her that he had come to Paris to work with her. She immediately asked him to report to her office, first thing the next morning, to join her team and this is why he has just come into her office, holding a drawing.]

If a colour is mentioned in respect of a furniture specification, Andrée Putman soon starts to explain how the dye was produced from lichen picked in the forest because of its similarity to the patina of copper. And, as conclusive proof of Eileen Gray's innate sense of elegance, Andrée Putman describes her intended meeting with her. After lengthy negotiations, she had been able to set up an appointment with this famous architect who no longer visited anyone. However, at the last minute, the meeting was cancelled. Andrée Putman later learned that, on the way, Eileen Gray had noticed a ladder in her stocking and could not bring herself to be seen in such a state. Andrée Putman hugs this precious anecdote about the celebrity to her heart like a secret, an anecdote which is, perhaps, more telling than the meeting might have been. This story is like a striking detail in a novella and, like all the other stories, proves that it is the way we look at reality which gives it this quality, this resonance. And this is how Andrée Putman works. Her buildings, which she visits like a traveller and a nomad throughout the world, can be read like a sequence of stories, stories without words, visual enigmas.

The ultimate paradox is that Andrée Putman's projects chronicle an elimination, the

Detail of lighting and mirror designed for the Carita Institute, Paris, 1988. Lights of ground glass and satin-finish nickel are set in strips into the ceiling and cornice of the room. The double-leafed mirror reflects more light into the room.

disappearance of something which previously existed and whose traces she forges into something which gives an impression of its former glory.

So it is not surprising that she compares her work to a story, that she tells the story of the past, of childhood, of passion and the story of the present, which has made her an "interior designer". This, however, is a title she rejects and it is true that she approaches the ever-critical issue of space, the shaping of emptiness, like a writer or a musician or a director; that is, with precision, humour, despair and perceptiveness, with that ability to digress, to invent, to laugh, and to add the secret and essential motifs which will give these buildings that quality of being correct, unalterable, or even of having always been there.

THE STORY OF THE PAST

CHILDHOOD AND MUSIC

Andrée Putman sometimes mentions her childhood and, when she does, she talks about really formative events, unforgettable impressions. This is the case with music which was her intended career.

"My sister and I were consolation prizes for our mother who was a wonderful artist, who played the piano all day long. We were difficult and over-emotional and, in the evening, she would play a certain piece of music which she knew would make us cry. She would play it with great depth of feeling, we would cry, she knew that and did it on purpose to heighten and quicken our sensitivity. We had been over-exposed to art. We sang in choirs and we were always going to museums (up to the age of 90, until it was impossible for her to get out of the house, my mother went to the Louvre every day). We would go to a concert every morning, before we were four. At ten, we could play incredibly complicated pieces and yet it is because I was not a virtuoso that I became interested in harmony and composition, for which I won first prize at the Paris Conservatoire, the highest award. This was how I lived, like an Egyptian mummy wrapped in bandages which prevented all movement or speech. I lived in this abstract, secret, incommunicable world of music, until that decisive point in my life when I won this prize, when I met the severe, spiteful, chilly gaze of the professor who presented it to me, saying 'Lock yourself in a room, buy reams of paper, hide yourself away for ten years and perhaps then you will manage to create a work.' He said this in a disgusted tone, as if he were punishing me. I gave up music there and then, just as I had won my way in, because that ridiculous caricature of the artist's work as a prison, the monastic idea of compulsory confinement, seemed unbearable.

"This unleashed a kind of whirlwind or frenzy of looking at paintings, architecture and the town around me, somewhat as if the spell which had kept me in music's thrall had been broken and I had finally reached the realm of sight.

My mother was equally passionate in her response to art and so I regained another part of my childhood, the endless trips to museums. I also recovered the heightened affinity with materials and colours possessed by my mother who, when financial disaster gradually overtook our family, had started to make our clothes herself. She did this with extraordinary talent and charm, despite her tendency to design clothes that could have been worn by the characters in the latest Virginia Woolf novel she had just finished reading, and the fact that our wonderful clothes were more like costumes than school uniforms. She was capable of summoning us to her room to finger the seventeenth-century ribbons which she kept hidden in a special chest, or of inventing games in which we had to sort out the ribbons depending on whether they were velvet, satin or silk. I was no stranger to this world of sight, having been prepared for it during the long summers we spent at Fontenay Abbey by a visual arousal bordering on a spiritual experience.

"I never really understood what a well-off family was doing at a Cistercian abbey, which seemed an unsuitable holiday venue and whose incongruity, of course, delighted me. One section of the abbey had been converted into a paper mill by my grandfather's family, who were descended from the Montgolfiers; the wallpaper, the teacups, the teapots and the shutters were covered with hot-air balloons, which added a further element of oddity to the brutal impact of all that space. For I was well aware that this place was too beautiful, too strange and too vast for anyone to emerge unscathed."

The importance of music and of Fontenay Abbey, therefore, can be seen in Andrée Putman's work. She refers to the strict discipline demanded by her music studies to explain the severity of her approach to architecture, which is an abstract and mathematical composition, while rhythm and harmony share similarities with the structure of space. Space, which is governed by the orchestration of vertical and horizontal planes, like the straight lines of the staves and the vertical layout of the notes on a page of music, is constructed around the concept of emptiness, in the same way that notes are defined by silence. The language of space is born out of a certain quality of emptiness.

EXPERIENCING EMPTINESS

Andrée Putman refers to emptiness in connection with an accidental fall she had one night on her way back from one of the choirs in which she was learning to sing. It was during the war, in the blackout, and in the thick, total darkness of the night, there was this void, this step forward into nothing. This was the first plunge and the first rift; it foreshadowed her abandonment of music at the age of twenty when, turning her back on her initial vocation and moving away from the isolated world of sound towards the world of colour and form offered by contemporary painting, she decided to empty her room completely. This decisive action was probably the outward sign of a rebellion against the established order and a deep-rooted change, but it was also her first look at space and her first act: the young Andrée

Putman threw out everything in the room, returning it to its original state, and then furnished it with an iron army bed, a bench by Bertoia and several paintings with unfamiliar and indecipherable signatures by distinguished artists that no-one had ever heard of, such as Bram van Velde and Alechinsky. On the bedside table, there were books by a writer at that time unread: Samuel Beckett.

THE DISCOVERY OF A GIFT

At the same time, Andrée Putman was working as a messenger, which gave her the opportunity to see a great deal and to meet many people. The journal she was working for was called *L'oeil* (The Eye), which she thought very apt; fate has a knack of playing games. She was soon asked to write about house interiors but, almost simultaneously, she met Denise Fayolle and became involved in a major project for Prisunic. Breaking the stranglehold of "good taste", and also of elitism and middle-class values, was not so far removed from that empty room and her eccentric parents, "themselves the black sheep of very wealthy, powerful French families; at school, they said to me that my parents had to be Russian or American". This also marked the beginning of a fresh revival of the ideas of the modern movement: using industrial machinery and mass distribution networks to produce "beautiful things for everyone". Andrée Putman initiated a daring venture: she persuaded the department stores to sell lithographs by Alechinsky, Bram van Velde, César, Arman and Messagier for little more than the price of a poster. But it was a little too early for the concept of art for everyone; it was the intellectuals who, when they got wind of the news, slummed it by going to Prisunic - which then became *the* place to shop - and snapped up these wonderful bargains at rock-bottom prices. Later, at the end of the sixties, still in collaboration with Denise Fayolle and Maïmé Arnodin, Andrée Putman was involved in the foundation of Mafia. This was a style consultancy, one of the first to create and establish the concept of product "communication", using events, shows and even parties, as well as research into packaging and the design of logos, to launch a product. In short, anything which was witty, intelligent, produced by art or recreation, was an excuse for trying something new. Everything could be invented and everything was possible: this was a time of short-lived and productive euphoria up to the end of the seventies, before the onset of recession and artistic sterility.

After working for Les Trois Suisses, the symbol of the popular logo, Andrée Putman left Mafia and launched another new venture: Créateurs et Industriels. Once again, this was based on an understanding and reinterpretation of the teachings of the Bauhaus movement, then the modern movement, applied to a different era: the meeting of arts and the convergence of disciplines, the possibility of initiating a dialogue and a free flow of ideas between the realms of fashion, cinema, painting and industry, and the attempt to combine technical expertise and art in a lasting union. The venue was a vast building, a former railway depot, paved with stone

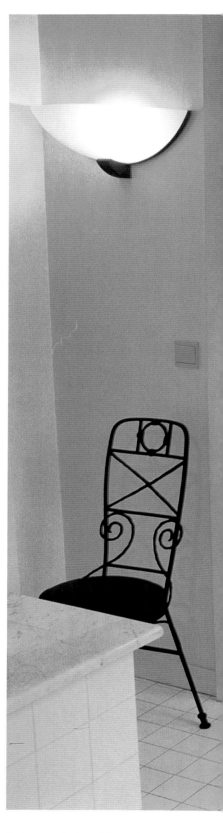

Bathroom designed for Daisy de Galard, Paris, 1982.

flags, crossed by metal cat-walks and illuminated by a huge glass roof. However, French manufacturers did not understand the timeliness of joining forces with the design world. At the very time when they should have been taking the risk of mass producing major lines, they "issued" several hundred examples of objects or clothes by Marc Held, Adeline André or Thierry Mugler, as they lacked the vision of the people who had involved them in this type of project. Even now, brilliant design is used in product display rather than in product policy, perhaps because the avant garde is incompatible with the tastes of the general public.

In the meantime, Andrée Putman had designed several homes for friends and had lived through some difficult years of austerity and solitude. She had a passion for rusty objects which she found at the flea market or in junk shops and, at the same time, she had begun to formulate the hazy idea that she perhaps had a talent for shaping that familiar emptiness and transforming it into a refuge - a term akin to the one she chose to describe the premises she opened, and where she more or less settled, in 1978: "écart", which conveys both the act of taking refuge and that of distancing oneself, after the fashion of the building on the rue Pavée, invisible to anyone who did not know it was there.

ECART AND THE REDISCOVERY OF MODERN ARCHITECTS

On the day of its opening, Ecart did not look anything like a showroom. It was in fact a place like no other, an oddity for its time, a former hangar transformed into a cathedral of light whose bare white walls emphasised reflections. The entrance was an anonymous black metal door, reached by going through the porch of an old block of flats in the Marais district. This building had no visible function, either private or public; it was like a house extension, containing an office and a telephone, where Andrée Putman worked to restore perplexing old-fashioned items, prototypes or unique objects which her unerring intuition had enabled her to find. There was furniture like the chair by Mallet Stevens, of which there were only four examples, or the chair by Herbst. There were also unlikely, yet authentic, documents, pieces or beginnings of half-finished objects which helped her start what she called her work "as an archaeologist-enthusiast of her own time" with surprises, wonders and finds like the discovery of the one version of Mariano Fortuny's lamp, at the back of a gloomy room in his Venetian palazzo, or the prototype of a trunk by Eileen Gray, which she found with the planks badly assembled at a cabinet-maker's shop in the rue Visconti. These were just a few of the pieces of furniture - standing alone, arranged like figures from a strange tribe, showered by light from the glass roof, in a building virtually impossible to find - which initiated the rediscovery of a crucial period in the history of architecture and design.

Andrée Putman is not yet fully aware of her gift for looking at objects and detecting their value, for understanding also the importance of light, the quality of a perspective. For this reason, she thinks that if ten people understand and buy the pieces of furniture that she reissues one by one, she will have fully attained her highly ambitious goal. "I realised, as early as '82-'83, that I was in the process of bringing international fame to those names that I had enthusiastically spelled out two years earlier. That is the greatest reward."

THE STORY OF THE PRESENT

Ecart has now become Ecart International and has moved premises by one street. The new building is true to itself, since the showroom is flooded with light from a glass roof and the old hoist from the former hangar is still there. Time has no dominion; Andrée Putman's style continues to be varied, and each modification, marked by the dates on the projects, adds to the uniqueness, the intensity of her vision, the precision of an internal line, of what Andrée Putman sometimes calls "the simple precision of a plumb-line". At the very height of her success, she remains an independent person who, in a way, renounced the idea of being tied - or of blindness - at the age of twenty and who travels the world tirelessly, building new homes with an eye to the places themselves, restoring their own characteristic ambience which she has rediscovered or invented, at times out of nothing at all. This is always a fresh act of creation, probably assisted by a sense of detachment which is both liberating and a burden, like a necessary task which is pressing and mysterious, demanding and problematic and which entails the utmost concentration on the smallest details, the same patient anxiety. "I needed a white with a hint of pale gold, like the faintest glitter of gold. And this research was anything but a matter of chance. There were moments of jubilation, when we thought we had found it, alternating with bouts of depression, when what should have been the final moment of discovery eluded us."

Using words, the unsubstantial stuff of stories, Andrée Putman elucidates her work as an interior designer, a "portraitist", taking several central themes as her guide.

EMPTINESS

"In my opinion, emptiness is, in a way, the reverse of emptiness. It is a word which always makes me picture a blank page: everything is possible. Creation is born out of it and sustained by it; emptiness is also connected with the idea of rebirth. Emptiness wipes out the past.

"There was that first blank page at twenty, when I cast myself adrift from the continent of music without having a new destination to head for. Then there was the second blank page of a new life - a woman alone who, during the time when she was not alone, had, from her window, coveted a printing works dating from the 1890s. This very distressing time, when I was confronted by all those wasted years, gave me the chance to start again with emptiness. Emptiness then becomes the spontaneous relinquishing of a collection of old objects which have ceased to mean anything. In a space devoid of meaning, it is better that the eye should skim over everything, that it should not actually be able to alight on anything. This emptiness

- which breeds silence - reveals what is strictly necessary: the bed, the reading lamp, the table, the chairs, and no other tables or objects, nothing. I had rehearsed this future scenario in a way when I was twenty but, since then, I had learned how to control emptiness. To rule over nothing is not so bad! And then, on another level, there is the emptiness of the theatre, the empty stage; sheer space and sheer potential for fiction. This is the way things happen when you are working.

"Making something empty means, to begin with, approximating to the true nature of a place, possibly rediscovering it, if the layers accumulated by time over the original architecture have distorted its integrity; unless, on the contrary, these transformations are an expression of its true nature, at times a strange and contradictory historical account. The choices are then arbitrary. In my opinion, a place is not predetermined by its original state - any input which I feel to be correct, genuine or necessary is worth keeping, in the same way that our input will, in its turn, become part of time's embellishment. Then, another type of emptiness sets in, our own *mise en scène*, as the dramatisation of emptiness is accomplished for us in various invisible ways. As in music, we are more concerned with the type of silence which is created between two notes and the way it reverberates against them, than by the notes themselves."

RHYTHM AND GEOMETRY

"Geometry is the branch of mathematics concerned with space, inscribed afterwards by light, but it is not necessarily synonymous with symmetry. Geometry, the concealed expression of structure, is the result of a lucid reading of space. Geometry does not exist in darkness. Geometry determines strength of line, the choice of axes, the plotting of reference points and is thereby rescued from the jumble of shadows where lines become indistinct. Within a space, you look for points of reference in the same way as you would in a town; and a town is the opposite of the wilderness, of the rambling and unreadable natural world where shapes such as a tree or a stone become in their turn recognisable signposts. It is important to establish guidelines for progression, just as the creation of perspectives guides the moving eye. The body is in direct contact with space. Oblique lines are discernible and experienced physically, like proportions and the scale of measurements between them. As for rhythm, this is the dimension of time which interrupts the orderliness of space. Rhythm is dynamic, it energises space, but it is the empty spaces between things which create rhythm; empty spaces, characterised by the openings made by windows and doors, and also by the different levels of depth which may occur between different planes, characterised by porticos, columns or any other features used in the construction and outline of buildings. So geometry which regulates space is fundamental to future freedom."

LIGHTING

"Light is the element which arouses sheer fascination: a vivid recollection of childhood impressions, of summer, of daylight, of the patches and bright flashes of southern light and sunshine, but above all the childlike fondness for light which holds darkness at bay. Today, in my work, it has become a game, a fake transmission of daylight, by using haloes, stripes and motifs designed to reflect its relationship with architecture. This may be the way it appears then disappears over the cornices, steps or perspectives but also in the way we use it like a completely distinctive material. Consequently, we will reverse the solid and the hollow parts of buildings, devise an opaque door framed by a luminous line, or emphasise the transition from floor to wall with a luminous skirting board which relieves and enhances the verticality. For the same reason, we often use shutters: the theme of light modulated and thickened by shadow, the play of shapes produced by a half-closed blind, casting you into the childlike world of random chance, which we try to reproduce like a secret language. Wanting to control light is akin to wanting to control a reverie, when a ray of light falls on a glass prism on my desk, showing me extraordinary patterns thrown on my ceiling. Light is infinitely varied when brought into contact with different materials. It can be variously filtered by a fabric, a fine wire mesh, ground glass or, on the contrary, it can be projected, in all its fierceness and clarity, against a metal surface. Light is the intangible substance which architecture captures and it is definitely no coincidence that each of my premises is characterised by the presence of overhead daylight. I have a constant memory of skies, visible in the town centre through sky lights or glass roofs. You lie down on a sofa and suddenly the sky, the stars, the dull light, the clouds are there, and the strangest thing of all is the tree branch, swaying in the wind, which moves in and out of your field of vision at regular intervals. These are the sort of impressions which haunt me when I am working, like magic lanterns and their entrancing images, or the thought that when you are playing with light, you are really playing with a star; magic lanterns like the ones described by Proust or Ingmar Bergman; the star as it was when I caught it slipping between the arches of the cloister at Fontenay Abbey."

COMPOSITION

"To an extent, the word 'composition' summarises what I look at most consistently: how is this done? What is the hidden structure behind each thing? At the back of a farm, a blind wall indicates windy weather conditions, and narrow loopholes instead of windows imply a connection with heat and sunlight. I like this realistic wisdom of builders. An airport like Roissy, for example, is built along such complicated lines that I still have not grasped the general plan, not in a discernible, internalised way, and yet the whole building is governed by the application of common sense. Common sense, when it arises from a fresh look at function must produce beautiful results, because any composition rooted in necessity, even created out

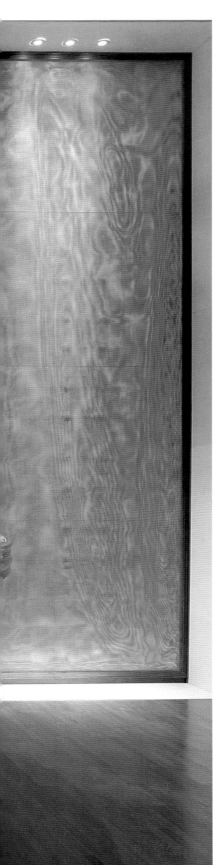

of nothing, is visually justifiable. However, composition is obviously an organisational factor, because it depends primarily on subversion, on skilful upheavals which are the result of complicated requirements. In this way, composition falls half-way between necessity and inventiveness. It would be interesting to know if an object, whether a piece of architecture, a painting, a piece of furniture, a sculpture, an airport or a farm, is instantly appealing because you understand how it is made or, on the contrary, because something will always baffle you. So, apart from questions of order, structure and construction, I realise that what catches my attention and guides me is not what I can see, but what baffles me. Our work on the exterior - proportions, masses, axes, perspectives, colours, materials and lighting - is actually a desire to make a statement about the interior, the interiority of emotion, of emptiness and of the inner scenography of space."

VOCABULARY

"Our vocabulary is primarily the one that my collaborators and I use in our stories. With each new project, we are there on site, or here in an office, taxing our imaginations. This is how many ideas, invoked by words, vanish again into the mists of oblivion: 'Look, picture a huge staircase - yes, but make it slightly curved to create a false perspective and give it a different length - or, alternatively, we could empty the space entirely and break it up with columns...' This is similar to a fairytale: everything is possible, and the stories we tell share the narrative structure of those infinite never-ending stories. Words and stories are our earliest exploratory tools. Sometimes, the story becomes strange, like that of the Le Lac Hotel in Japan, when we were assailed by the deepest feeling of dismay when we saw the site: at the edge of a lake, with surroundings resembling a building site, a dead-end place, half-industrialised and destined for some sort of future town-planning programme. So we told the story of an upside-down building, as though reflected on the surface of the lake. For the first time we used Kool Shade, which we had until then adapted for other purposes, in its original form. This material is made of very thin copper slats, miniaturised blinds intended to be used instead of air conditioning. We enclosed the building in this fine metallic light-sensitive casing, so as to cut off the view from the rooms, filtering it to make the landscape seem veiled, while from the outside, this second skin masked the sinister reality of the building itself. But this is not the first time that these things have happened and they obviously give us the opportunity to pursue unforeseen solutions further. When the contractors took me to see Morgans Hotel in New York and they stopped on the way, on the pavement opposite a second-rate hotel, an old ramshackle hotel, I looked at them, slightly surprised that we had stopped, and asked them: 'Where's the hotel? Is it far?' They replied, pointing over the road, 'That's it': incontrovertible proof that everything is possible and that there is nothing inevitable about interior design. Furthermore, Morgans Hotel is one of the buildings in which we made the most extensive use

Detail of the bar in the restaurant
designed for Ebel at the Basel
Trade Fair in 1986.

of contrasts. The contrast between gloss and matt, smooth and rough, transparent and opaque, white and black, contrasting textures, expensive materials and inexpensive materials."

THE MATERIALS

"Materials almost always have an opposite. It is often the bizarre incompatibility between two materials, which were not meant to be seen together, that creates a thought-provoking effect. I like laying a Roman glass mosaic in smooth cement, or touching up a piece of wood, showing off the veins with a patina which is not generally used with it and which makes the pattern stand out more clearly. Materials are not objective, like letters in a vocabulary; they have connotations, they belong to a code, like shapes or words. 10 x 10cm stoneware tiles inevitably bring to mind council housing. I am interested in overturning this categorisation of materials, in adapting them, obliterating the depressing image that stoneware has by adding some gold-coloured molten glass which transforms it, wipes out its past and sheds new light on it as a whole. We may also have occasion to use it as a border, so as to break up a surface, and then we use it as tastefully and as sparingly as if it were one of the most expensive, valuable materials. I think that this form of freedom is one of the fundamental aspects of our work and in reality comes down to a continual statement of doubt: are we convinced that a wash-basin should have the top of a wash-basin? What if, for example, it was more like a small bowl, perched like a heron? We like to meddle with the shapes and sizes of everyday objects, to design doors which are too big or too small, too high or too narrow, to discover new approaches, unrestricted by the automatic attitudes dictated by the 'standard' approach."

WATER AND FIRE

"In apartments designed by Haussmann, a 50-metre-long corridor goes all the way through to an isolated kitchen while near the rooms, with a little luck, a tiny bathroom sports the ample dimensions of a period bathtub. I think this is a strange layout. Personally, I prefer bathrooms which, according to my own geography, have more in common with the Greek and Roman baths; that is, with having an indispensable and healthy session of purification by water, a comforting system of symbols communicated by materials such as tiles, lighting and an unlimited supply of water. This is a time when you can care for your body, undisturbed by ceremony or display, surrounded by the many soothing details essential for that moment of truth when you take off all your clothes and look at yourself severely, at times unsympathetically. The mirror provides time for reflection, not simply the reflection of an image in a mirror, but also an indication of the mind which is sceptical about being indistinguishable from the precarious image facing it. It is strange that water, which is naturally so untrammelled and limitless, should be so curbed and channelled, as if neutralised, in the town, which is, like our bodies, relentlessly governed by contemporary requirements for health and mandatory aesthetic appeal. The bathroom is the only irreplaceable room in the house, along with the kitchen. These two nerve centres are exiled by the modern allocation of space and by everyday activities, as if they had acquired the reputation of being unwelcome guests. Domestic waste disposal is another thorny subject, not because we should pay particular attention to it, but because its systemic and organised elimination says a great deal about our need to conceal our insect-like condition as fast as possible; a condition which, if true, would mark us as frail, short-lived creatures. So, on the contrary, for this reason, I believe that the closest attention should always be paid to the bathroom and the kitchen, the seat of water and fire, where the ancient and laughable drama of human life is played out, interspersed by the repeated actions of using water for washing and fire for cooking. This would ensure that these rooms offer the vital level of physical comfort essential for our spiritual ease."

Comfort

"My idea of comfort has very little to do with tea-cosies, quilted curtains and wool carpets. I am not especially concerned with how plump an armchair is. I think visual comfort is far more important than physical comfort. The state of emptiness I tried to achieve when I was twenty, a sort of disorientation which startles you out of sleep is, in my opinion, connected with this idea of mental and visual comfort, more necessary than the anaesthetising effect of cosy surroundings. For what is being called into question is this notion of ignoring bodily discomfort, supported by theories like ergonomics, which I more or less ignore. Things which have been designed are never soft and, in my opinion, comfort is the use of design to build on what is organic, rather than to expunge it with softness and flabbiness. Is it really so comfortable to allow things to become heavier and more unwieldy? On the other hand, I think that there is nothing more comfortable than having a place to put away your boots when you come in from a muddy walk, or having a spice within arm's reach at the precise moment you need it for something you are cooking, or being able to switch on a light that illuminates the hand which is writing on the sheet of paper, without throwing a shadow. This ability to understand actions is important to me and interests me. When I was a child, I read about the adventures of Patapouf and Filifer. Patapouf slept in a four-poster bed and when he woke up, he needed only to stretch out his hand to pick one of the countless flavours of ice-cream distributed by a special machine next to his bed. Filifer slept on the pipes of the stove and when he woke up, a trapdoor opened automatically, tumbling him into a basin of iced water in which he had a quick wash before going to work. Let's say that I would rather be Patapouf when it comes to bathrooms and Filifer for everything else!"

DISCIPLINE AND MADNESS

"Be steady and well-ordered in your life, so that your work can be fierce and original."

Andrée Putman quotes this sentence from Flaubert with a smile, and sitting very straight at her black semi-circular desk she silently closes the silver lid of her cigarette case which goes everywhere with her.

She crosses time steadily, as if using the endlessly repeated lines of the musical staves which hold the notes as stepping stones. But, like Giacometti, she is aware that the distance between the wing and the bridge of the nose is infinite, similar to a wilderness which is perhaps impossible to cross.

"What interests me", she says, "is the gap between discipline and madness." Few things can express this idea as well as the work directly opposite her, a painting by Jean-Pierre Raynaud, composed of white squares measuring 20x20 mm, a square space very rigidly delineated by the geometry of the squares arranged in it. At their base is the aftermath of a landslide, a demolition or an earthquake: a formless mass of squares, identical but broken, crumbling, disused pieces threatened by gritty disintegration.

The striking dialectic which dominates this image successfully fulfils its purpose in its direct presentation of a paradox: order and disorder, the will to build and chaos. And in this gap, not at one or other of the poles, but in the space which both joins and separates them, what might be called chance has free rein; chance, that instrument of fate, about which Andrée Putman says, "Strangely, chance is an immensely comforting thought, like a window giving on to a miracle, the meeting of two contrasting and independent worlds, the fragile certainty that things have a meaning."

Detail of a desk designed for the director of a private company in Belgium. It is made of black polished metal and black-stained oak with bronze details.

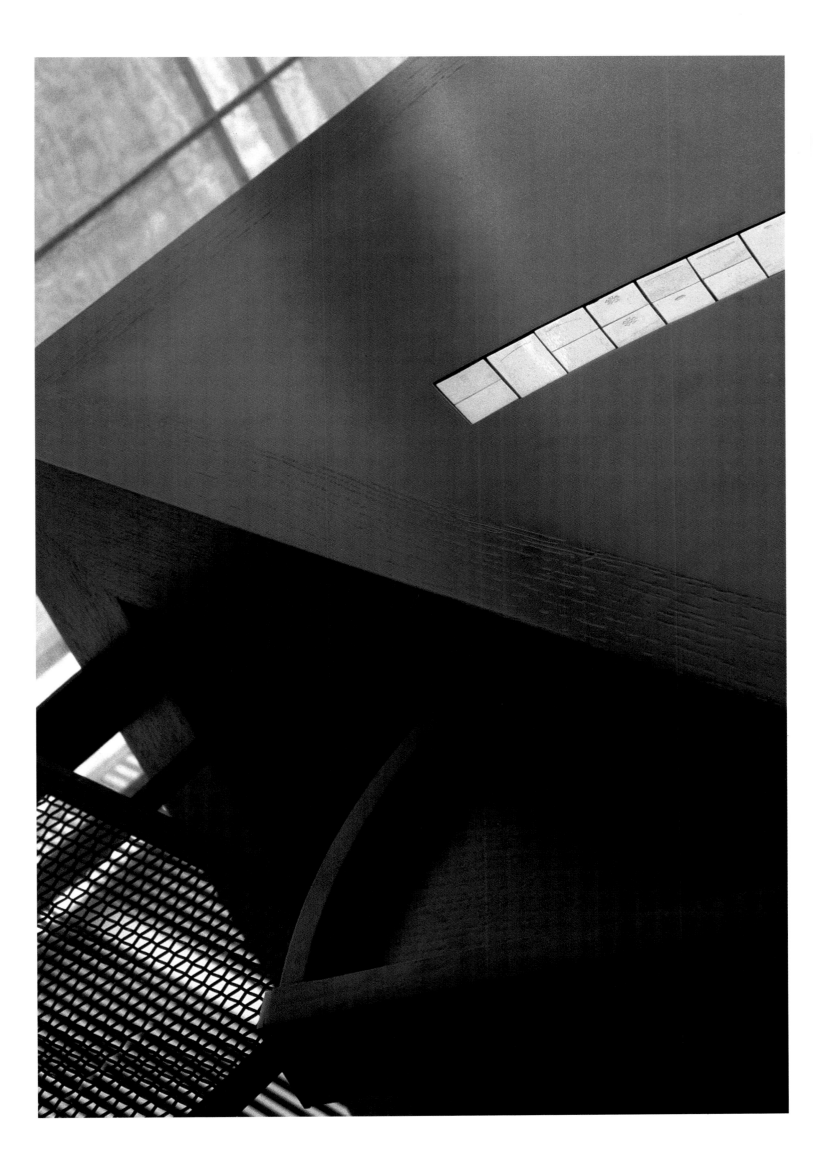

Le Voyage
l'immobili

IN TRANSIT AND AT REST

A hotel is a contradictory place. It is the unknown and distant
destination we reach after a long journey. But for that very
reason, it should be a familiar place, resembling a house
without parodying it, a refuge, a place of rest. On the subject
of hotel bathrooms, Andrée Putman recalls a short story by
Katherine Mansfield in which the horrified heroine discovers a
hairpin in the washbasin. This hairpin, the inoffensive but
glaring reminder of the past life of the place, an anonymous
and therefore unsettling presence, represents, on the contrary,
the hotel's quintessential nature: a space which is always
potential, timeless, both strange and familiar. So, beyond the
conceptual issues of architectural relationships, the allocation
and structuring of space, Ecart's work is primarily concerned
with thoughtful touches, solicitous ideas: a small easily
reached shelf for your keys near the door, soft lighting for tired
eyes, colour schemes which gradually reveal inconspicuous
motifs, unobtrusively worked into the texture of the fabrics,
and surprises in the composition of masses, which make you
think that each room may be different. In the bathroom,
there are a plethora of considerate details: a heated towel-rail,
modulated, sympathetic lighting and concealed mirrors. All
are tokens of comfort essential for a period of acclimatisation
and tranquillity between two places, two destinations, two
venues.

PREVIOUS SPREAD

MORGANS HOTEL,
New York (1984)

A corner room in Morgans Hotel,
looking out on to Madison
Avenue.

The conversion of Morgans Hotel was the first in a long list of projects for which it was, to a certain extent, the catalyst. The project was simply, however, to reconsider what a hotel should be: neither consecrated to the uniform, chilly luxury of international hotels, nor imprisoned in an out-of-date style of décor with enormous flowers and wallpaper, but intended for the traveller in search of rest and privacy. The rooms were designed with this in mind, offering the comfort of natural, simple materials with several pieces of furniture and re-editions, and shades of colour distinguished by scarcely visible textures. The bathrooms, in black and white tiles, alluding to the trend set by the Vienna Secession at the turn of the century, contain abundant bathroom linen and the mystery of Eileen Gray's mirror.

In the lobby the pattern on the floor is echoed in the carpet. The walls are made up of painted glass panels, framed with bronze-coloured brass. The furniture is of tubular steel and grey leather.

MORGANS HOTEL

The walls of one of the bathrooms, shown left, are chequered with black and white ceramic tiles measuring 10 x 10cm. Accessories, including the grey metal basins, mirrors and white porcelain soap dishes, were designed for the project by Ecart. • All the bedrooms have a large recessed window, framed by reconstituted maple panelling, below left. The armchair is modelled on a design by Hoffman. • The vanity unit in this room, right, is in grey Colorcore. The chair is by Mallet-Stevens, and the lamp is from the Bureau de Commerce.

MORGANS HOTEL,
New York (refurbishment:1996)

The challenge in this project was to modernise the décor of a hotel whose fame brooked very little change. It is fascinating to see how Ecart revamped this site, designed and conceived by Andrée Putman and her team twelve years earlier, by making some virtually infinitesimal modifications. These included: "moving from a chilly grey to a pinkish mole-grey, choosing corduroy velvet for the armchairs instead of the striped flannel of men's suits. The black and white chequered coverlets are replaced by warm sand-coloured coverlets, and the duvet covers and the headrests are patterned with tiny, almost invisible, designs. The only major change, in the lobby, is the inclusion of a varied assortment of worn old armchairs." Creating the impression that certain objects have always been here, subtly restoring the balance between different concepts of time, between new objects which are unobtrusively flawless and old objects which have insinuated themselves into the present, this project encapsulates the art of continuity.

The lobby, seen from the entrance to the elevator, is furnished with antique leather club chairs. In the centre is the glazed entrance vestibule.
• A typical guestroom, shown left, has a built-in day bed below the window. The sleek armchairs are covered in thick corduroy.

SAINT JAMES CLUB,
Paris (1986)

The furniture in the Saint James Club is of stained and limed ash. The room shown far left contains a roll-top desk and a table which can be wound up or down. • The jacuzzi is lit by a concealed strip above the cornice and wall lights made of ground glass and nickel-plating. Its surround is of Carrara marble. The walls are covered with white ceramic tiles, measuring 10 x 10cm, with a border of blue and black glazed tiles. Grey stoneware tiles measuring 5 x 5cm cover the floor. • In one of the bathrooms, above, wash basins are set into Carrara marble. Tiny glazed tiles decorate the walls. Fittings include a Pyrex and nickel towel rail, Brot mirrors and wall lights by Christopher Wray. The large mirrors are held in place by strips of nickel.

29

WASSERTURM HOTEL,
Cologne (1990)

This former water tower, a listed historical monument although badly damaged during the war, was in fact already structured in the way its spaces were allocated at the time of its restoration and proposed conversion into a hotel. The interior design programme involved creating 80 rooms within this huge tower made up of nine brick storeys and structured by arches. The inner masses were determined by the outer openings: sometimes high ogive windows, sometimes tiny bull's-eye windows. The basic principle behind the conversion was determined by the constraints imposed both by the scale and by the lighting, which varied from dazzling brightness to darkness, and consisted of designing split-level rooms with illuminated dividing walls when there was no available natural light. Each room was completely planned around the more Cartesian spaces created by the interior fittings. These develop the interesting aspects of the arc of a circle (straight lines unfolding in a fan shape in the axis of a curve) but avoid its strangeness. The deliberate softness and uniformity of the materials and colours are in direct contrast to the graphic, severe appearance of the spaces at the centre of the tower, whose original brickwork has been preserved.

The tower was constructed by the British engineer Charles Moore between 1868 and 1872 and is the largest water tower in Europe.
• An unusual view of the centre of the hall from the second floor, right, shows the mysterious passages which lead to the guestrooms.

WASSERTURM HOTEL

In this duplex suite the bedroom is reached by a circular staircase.

33

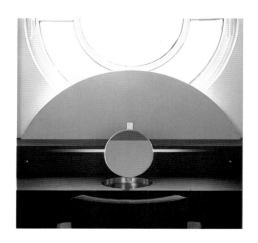

WASSERTURM HOTEL

A bedroom, above, in one of the suites. Elements used in other parts of the hotel, such as luminous walls and wall sconces, have been included here to give a continuity to the building.
• A semi-circular console which follows the curve of the vault around a bull's-eye window can serve as a desk or, through the use of a mirror that can be stood upright, as a dressing table. A semi-circular screen can be pulled up at night to cover the porthole window. • In the bathroom, a curved niche resembling a fountain serves as a sink. It is made from ceramic tiles in two sizes: 2 x 2cm and 5 x 5cm.

LE LAC HOTEL,
Kawaguchiko-Cho (1988)

*This project was initially
presented as the conversion of a
hotel at the foot of the
legendary Mount Fuji beside a
sun-drenched lake; however, the
reality of the location turned out
to be completely different: an ill-
considered town-planning
programme; a vast, rambling
urban construction site scattered
with clusters of ramshackle
housing. The project of
designing a luxury hotel in a
devastated site became a
struggle against all odds. Ecart,
therefore, decided on an
aggressive course of action: to
shut out the real world by
enclosing the building in Kool
Shade, a very fine copper veil,
which both came between the
hotel and the world outside and
created an "inner space". This
paradox is continued by the
rooms, which had to solve the
difficulties caused by their
dimensions (very long and
narrow); each is actually an
immense bathroom, separated
from the bed by two screens,
which, once again, reverse the
positive and negative effects of
light. The bathroom is like a
temple of beauty where the
washbasin stands like an altar in
front of a window of opaque
glass. Light is of paramount
importance in this hotel which
superimposes the various
transparent partitions, from the
outer casing to the screens, in
subtle variations, so that it is an
opaque building during the day
and transparent at night.*

The hotel exterior, which was
constructed by fixing black Kool
Shade screening on to the existing
building. • The main door is of
antique bronze panels mounted
on glass.

37

LE LAC HOTEL

*A view of the main door from the
entry hall. The seating is of
horsehair and the carpet runner is
wool with bronze studs.*

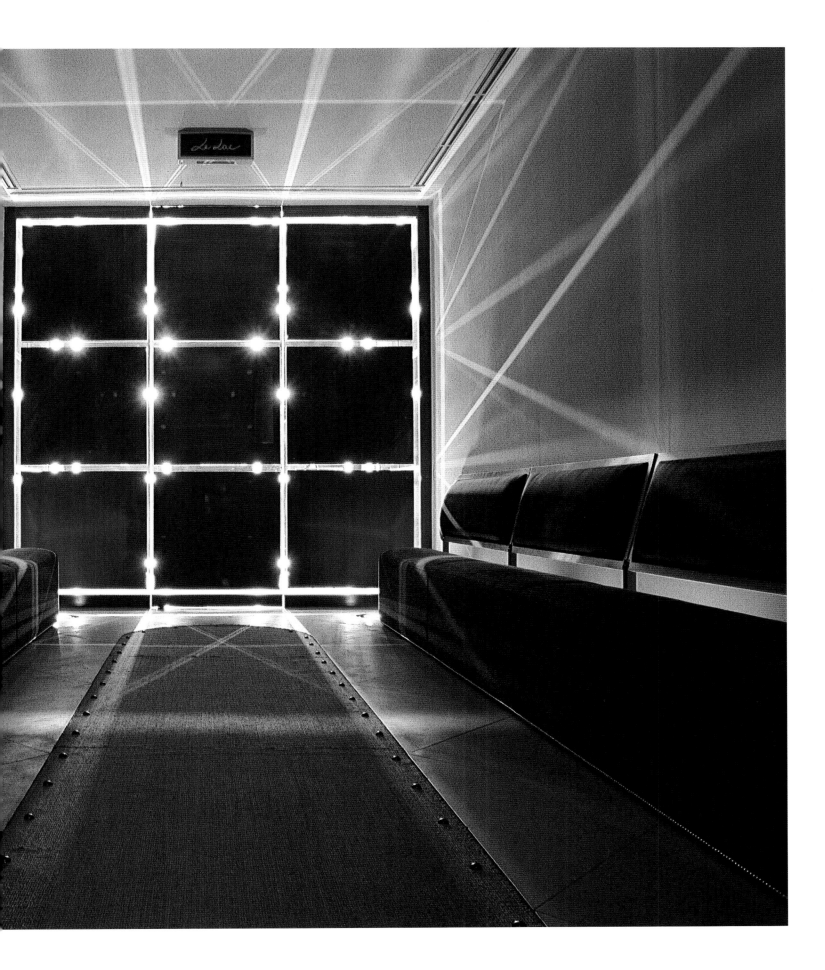

LE LAC HOTEL

In a typical room a Monsanto PVC
translucent glass screen with a
nickel-plated frame divides off the
bathroom. The bath and side
table are of grey ceramic tiles, and
the bed frame is oak. The
armchairs and sofa are by Ecart.
• A double sink in the bathroom,
far right, consists of a pre-formed
polished concrete bowl and a
stand of glass mosaic tiles. The
sliding glass screen is of Monsanto
PVC translucent glass with flush-
mounted mirrors. There are
recessed lights in the bull-nose
end walls.

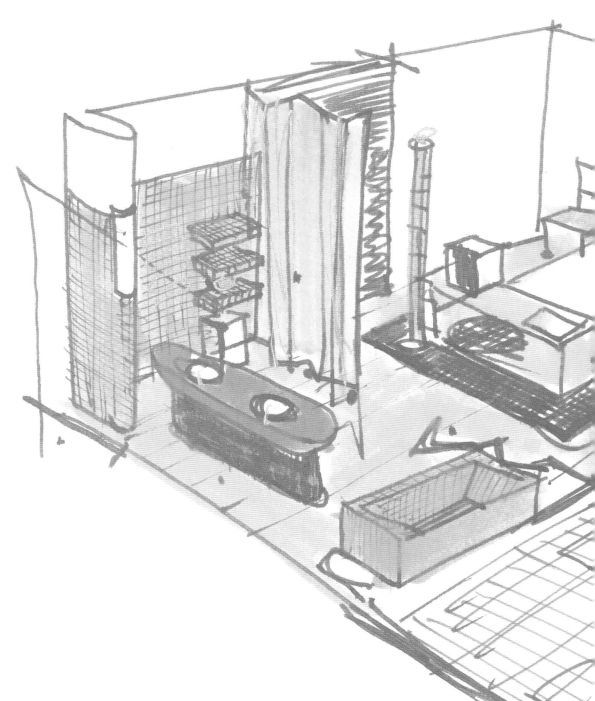

THE ORCHID CLUB HOUSE, Kobé (1992)

In Kobé, Japan, a block of residential buildings built by Charles Moore is designed in such a way as to preserve semi-private reception areas on the ground floor which enable visitors to be entertained without infringing the intimate privacy of the home. Lounges and a restaurant and bar were therefore the functions which needed to be accommodated in a vast rectangle of 400 m², next to a garden. The project, which opens with a door seemingly formed of sea-spray, a mysterious, vertical froth of bubbles, in homage to the aquarium given to Andrée Putman by Bob Wilson, in the Ecart showroom, is basically designed as a barrier: posts which structure and break up the space at regular intervals. The illuminated glass panels, in bronze frames, can be wound up and down at will, enabling the view to be blocked or revealed. Curves, which are reminiscent of a swelling wave, are counter-balanced by the theme of squares which orders the surfaces: Versailles parquet flooring, table units which feature a square balanced on end like a diamond, and a coffered ceiling. At the back, a bar, in the same way as the rest of the space, plays on the relationship between semi-darkness and half-light, with thin strips of light emphasising the horizontal lines.

The entry door to the Club House, which is 10cm thick, consists of a sheet of synthetic glass in a metallic frame. The transparent liquid inside it creates the effect of a curtain of bubbles. It opens automatically by means of a photo-electric cell. • A luminous glass screen is a striking feature of the main salon, right. The floor is Versailles oak parquet, covered with wool rugs by Ecart. The floor lamps are by Kalida, and the sofa by Jean-Michel Frank. The "Half-Moon" table is of Wenge wood.

SHERATON HOTEL,
Roissy (1995)

Situated in a surreal landscape, at the foot of the landing runways, the hotel, built by architect Paul Andreux, looks like a huge liner set down in a vista of sky and roads. "Its geographical location makes it the quintessential hotel or half-way house, a place for spending several hours, at most a night, in transit between two destinations." The rooms, done out by Ecart in restful colours, shades of fawn, sand, beige, grey and taupe, offer a warm welcome to weary travellers passing through. Materials, wood and light are combined to create a neat and comfortable environment. A huge circular wooden "tower" conceals the functional elements: television, bar, crockery and accessories. In front of the windows is a desk where you can write a letter or work and, when you look up, contemplate the strange sight of the planes which seem to have been abandoned on the runways like toys. Echoing the theme that the skies are the limit, which is highlighted by both your surroundings and the transience of time, huge pictures comprising photographs of clouds and small toys, like the view from a plane window, create the sensation of speed.

Gangways on several floors. The room doors are of oak with Persian blinds. Guardrails are made of graduated sanded glass, with oak handrails. The wall lights are illuminated stars: an electrical device is recessed into the wall and covered with a white, blue or green sanded glass star.

One of the bedrooms, shown above, is furnished with a chair and matching footstool in suedette. A bentwood cherry tower with a sliding door houses the television and bar. The luggage stand and small table are also made of cherry. On the wall is a photograph by J. Schlomoff. • In front of the window, right, is a handsome desk space. A built-in mirror transforms this desk into a dressing table. • Above left, detail of a wall light in the gangway and a room number.

SHERATON HOTEL

The rooms, reached by
long gangways that
liberate space and provoke
feelings of vertigo, are
similar to large "cabins"
on an ocean-going ship.
In the lobby, a large blue
rug, depicting the milky
way studded with
shooting stars, contributes
to the interplay between
blue and the night. This
is picked up in vast
illuminated, opalescent
areas which call to mind
the diffuse radiance of
clouds. The space is
anchored by the use of
heavy, polished dark
wood, an allusion to the
great English hotels and a
reference to a past which
lurks here in this place
dedicated to the nomadic
spirit of modern life, to
journeys and to waiting.

In the lobby, an illuminated
striated, convex glass pod
conceals the technical units
and the lifts. The floor is
covered with Savoie marble
flags.

AIR FRANCE, CONCORDE
(1993)

"With this project", said Andrée Putman, "our fundamental aim was to show that passengers are enjoying the luxury of a magnificent time-saving machine. In a plane, the themes of time and space are almost infinite for the former and extremely restricted for the latter." These perceptions, generated by the fastest form of travel available to us today, are translated by "the aim of removing all signs of frivolity, of self-importance, and replacing them with a more appropriate symbol of authority, that of elegance". Subtly enlarging the capacity of the luggage compartments makes it possible to gain some height and space, while a variety of simple details, which come into their own during the flight, guarantee an extremely high level of passenger comfort. These include white piqué headrest covers, cashmere travelling rugs and table linen to accompany the first-class meals. The central aisle runner parades the geometric motif of a brilliant blue border.

Seats are covered in finely-striped grey and taupe ottoman, with removable headrest covers made of white cotton piqué. Cutlery is laid out on a pure linen table mat.
• Salt and pepper shakers pick up the motif of the border of the plane's central aisle runner. A linen serviette is rolled in corrugated Kraft.

A general view of the interior of the plane. • In the central aisle, the soothing, neutral colours of the seats and walls are set off by the beige and blue border of the aisle runner.

La représentation

REPRESENTATION AND EXECUTION

When interior design represents a name, a logo, it is actually an exercise in portraiture: how the identity of a business or a company can be communicated by the use of its most abiding aspects, those which attract visitors before they have even spoken to anyone. This task is poles apart from the work done on galleries, for example, and entails specific historical research and the translation of this information into the language of form; although often, the products on display must also be given the freedom to wield their own evocative power, which is then echoed by the interior design. Portraying a logo, or the person behind the logo, may also mean arranging personal objects, like pictures, at intervals around the exhibition space, or providing a space which is sufficiently flexible to allow its image, which is not fixed, to be changed or modified.

PREVIOUS SPREAD

THE WEXNER CENTER,
Columbus (1992)

The entry to the exhibition is through the Chinese shadow room, with its back-lit curvilinear Mylar screen with hanging cardboard cut-outs. The dress is by John Galliano.

Ecart was asked to provide the mise en scène for the exhibition "60 years of Haute Couture - in Black and White", at the Wexner Center for the Arts in Columbus, Ohio. The immediate decision was to block off all daylight to create an imaginary world of the past revisited. The exhibition space was designed like a labyrinth and each subsequent room displayed different costumes and also the workshops of the time, recreated, with work tables, cloth patterns, pins and wooden mannequins. As time stood still, in a dreamlike atmosphere, "scenes" and "tableaux" unfolded, haunted by vanished people, on a journey back into the depths of time, illustrating the paradox of fashion, a transient thing which is held constant outside of reality by the art of museography.

In the little black dress section, the rear wall shows an enlarged and distorted version of Marcel Duchamp's Nude Descending a Staircase.

SHOWROOM FOR ECART,
Paris (1992)

The Ecart showroom and offices in Paris are anything but ostentatious. They convey perfectly the work of the drawing office by being simultaneously neutral and distinctive, recognisable without the help of any excessive gestures or irrelevant details. The architecture, which is arranged according to masses, is determined to a large extent by the glass roof. On the ground floor, there is an uncluttered area, free of obstacles, in full daylight, for the display of furniture and re-editions, with small rooms and offices, which appear or disappear behind high sliding doors; while upstairs, on the other side of the paved courtyard, there are the main offices, spacious white rooms accentuated by details like metal plinths and wide strips of parquet flooring, which contain the tranquillity and light so essential for concentration. The simultaneously complicated, abstract and natural space of this building, which provides a sequence of different views and perspectives, is actually symmetrical and strictly in proportion. It widely develops the theme of high doors, a frequently-repeated principle, which gives the building a lofty simplicity.

The completed alterations at Ecart, left. The hoist is the only remaining trace of the recent past. Bob Wilson designed the aquarium, Fortuny the reflector.
• In Andrée Putman's study, above, Jean-Pierre Raynaud's Golden Archetype (1989) is displayed on a wooden stand. The drawings are by Olivier Thome and the carpet was designed by Andrée. The shell-shaped sofa upholstered in plush silk velvet once belonged to Paul Morand.
• The stairwell at Ecart, right, has a sliding door of Monsanto glass.

OFFICES FOR ECART

This room is defined by a curved
screen of gauze netting. The walls
are of the original stone. The
furniture includes a "Tectona"
bench and small chairs by Mallet-
Stevens. Porcelain designed by
Andrée Putman is displayed on
luminous shelves.

EBEL STAND, Basel (1986)

This was a short-term, small-scale (300 m²) project. The brief was to construct a stand for Ebel, the watch manufacturer, for the Basel trade fair. It was decided to achieve "emphasis through disappearance", by devising a white unit, an opaque piece of architecture with a narrow slit cut lengthwise into the side in which five or six watches were exhibited, each illuminated by a pencil of light. At the side, a disproportionately large door led to a theatre-like corridor where small isolated offices allowed visitors to be entertained in intimate, comfortable surroundings. At the back of the stand, there was a high-quality restaurant. The dramatic, minimalist treatment and the "brutal" effect of the architecture - in short, the work done on scale and perspective - transformed the stand into a piece of theatre and a sculpture. The Ebel shops, which take their design from variations on this initial image, pick up the massive portico and the concept of a piece of architecture functioning as a jewel-box.

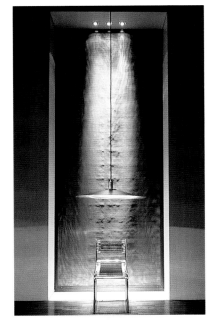

The exterior of the stand, above left, was constructed from lacquered wood cladding, with recesses of frosted glass and dull bronze details. • The pewter top of the restaurant bar, below left, was decorated with an embossed guilloche pattern. The recesses behind it contained grey gauze netting over ground glass, giving the appearance of watered silk.
• The stand, above right, was furnished with chairs by René Herbst. The table had a ground glass top which was lit from above and below. Safes were hidden behind the medium-density-fibreboard panels.
• Hanging lights, below right, in the restaurant could be raised or lowered.

**EBEL SHOWROOM,
Hardhof (1990)**

*A detail of the staircase in the
Hardhof showroom, opposite,
showing the corroded metal
banister. • At the entrance, left, is
a luminous bar in frosted glass
with a pewter top. The walls and
ceiling are panelled with leather,
divided by deep, luminous
grooves, and the floor is covered
with Haltoplex. The sliding door is
of metal and frosted glass. • The
conference room/film theatre,
below, has luminous walls made
of wire mesh and frosted glass.
The ceiling is grey-lacquered. The
horsehair chairs are by Mallet-
Stevens.*

VIA EXHIBITION,
Paris (1990)

The challenge was to set the scene at the Musée des Arts Décoratifs in Paris for 10 years of furniture design (within the framework of VIA, an institution devoted to the development of furniture innovation), without stacking up dozens of chairs and tables. To meet this challenge, Ecart decided to create a chronological progression, divided into sequences - a series of dramatised events: a tower of one-off seats; a Chinese shadow-room; a multitude of "Ara" stools by Philippe Starck on which to sit to watch a video depicting 10 years of activity in the furniture industry; backdrops for design - small, stylised alcoves in which objects were displayed and highlighted. The progression travelled through time, like a reading, looking at high points and periods of uncertainty, given substance by the play of shadow and light, of illusion and entertainment.

The video room, far left, is filled with "Ara" stools by Philippe Starck. The cube is of frosted glass, and the wall is hung with gauze netting. • A wall in laminate, left, created specially for the exhibition. The furniture stands in gold-painted chipboard recesses.

L'efficacité

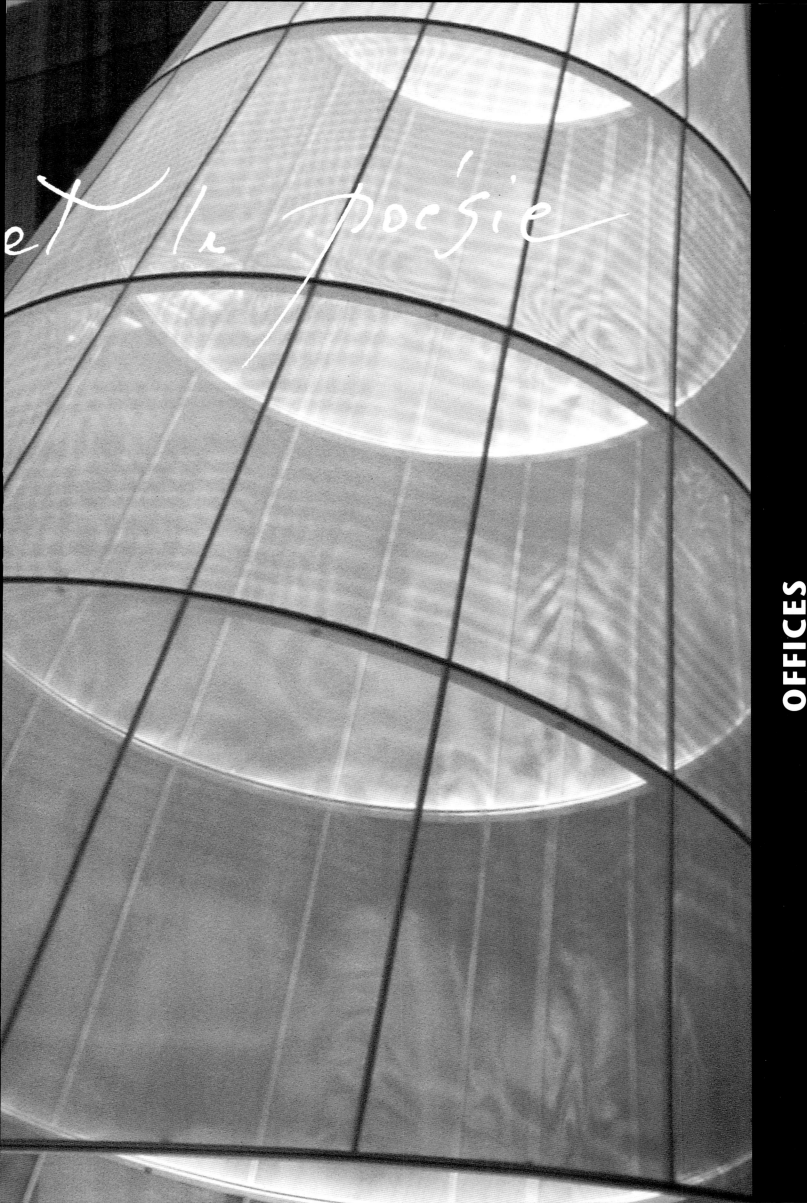

et la poésie

EFFICIENCY AND POETRY

Ecart's work always deals to an extent with the paradox of designing thoroughfares for private places. An office is, of course, devoted to concentration, to work, to public life, to efficiency and to a certain type of corporate identity. It is, however, also a place which does not have to be condemned to the anonymity of a cold, modern, international style. An office could also mirror its owner. It could make the most of the softness of a material, of a colour, or a concealed object to promote peace of mind. The obligatory spirit of "performance" which gives an overly regulated environment the stamp of neutrality could instead be communicated by choice and a certain style of décor.

The desire to fulfil a specific and unusual need is one of the central precepts governing the work of the drawing office. An office could therefore simply be the most welcoming area, conducive to thought; also the place where people often spend more time than they do at home, a place which at times will be occupied from dawn until dusk.

PREVIOUS SPREAD

OFFICES FOR LA SEPT,
Paris (1991)

Detail of the entrance hall of the La Sept offices showing the cone above the reception desk which consists of a light beam shaded by white gauze netting.

This project was to design some offices within the framework of a piece of unappealing modern architecture. Ecart therefore put forward the design of a rather spectacular lobby, a symbolic hall, in which the logo of the seventh French television channel, La Sept, figured prominently. As is often the case, thoughts are generated by memories and powerful images. Hence the appearance of a beam of white light, like the one which travels over the music-hall stage, as if "tracking"; a beam which becomes a strange, powerful and oblique object, seeming to move over the reception desk and which, although it looks off-centre, is the focal point of the composition. Furthermore, the shelters, which Andrée Putman had come across on a deserted windy beach in the north of France, were transformed into comfortable seats, similar to small three-sided houses, from which the visitor is able to watch the programmes on the television screens. La Sept, with its different shades of blue, the colour of a television when switched on, becomes transparent and luminous at night.

The entrance hall, left, has a granite slab floor and black metallic walls with gauze netting screens and Kool Shade. The reception desk, sofas and television cabinets are of Nexxitel, and the trees are limes. • The corridors, above, are carpeted with Andrée Putman's lichen moquette. The recessed wall lights are of sanded glass, and the sofa is of grey canvas. • The president's office, right, is furnished with a stained oak desk, a wire mesh and gauze netting screen, an armchair by Mallet-Stevens and a lamp by Fortuny.

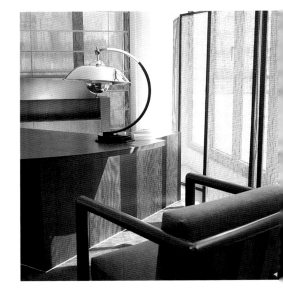

OFFICE FOR M. JACK LANG,
Paris (1984)

The office of the Minister for Culture. The half-moon desk measures 3m in diameter and matches the low table in two halves made of sycamore and bronze-coloured metal. The small armchairs are of natural leather with ivory piping.

HOTEL DE REGION,
Bordeaux (1987)

The reception room of the Hôtel de Région, left, contains low tables in epoxy metal and sanded glass, and armchairs by Ecart Design. • The office and sitting room for M. Jacques Chaban-Delmas, right, contains a limed-oak desk and mole-grey leather armchairs. The curtains are pleated white taffeta, and circular woollen rugs cover the oak floor. The domed ceiling light is made of ground glass with a nickel reflector, and more lights are set into slits in the pillars. The desk lamp is by Fortuny. One side of the room is oak-panelled.

VILLA TURQUE,
La Chaux de Fonds (1988)

*The exterior of Le Corbusier's
Turkish House at La Chaux de
Fonds, Switzerland. • Bookcases
concealed behind illuminated
fronts support Le Corbusier's
pediment. • A view of the sitting
room from the first floor. The
Roman blinds are of fine net and
silk.*

VILLA TURQUE

The furniture on the first floor includes a grey raw oak vanity unit. The wall lights are of nickel and frosted glass. • The walls of the conference room/film theatre are of grey-painted panelling, with wall lights of nickel and frosted glass. The doors are covered in horsehair. The leather swivel chairs are by Le Corbusier.

OFFICE FOR THE MINISTRY OF FINANCES, Bercy (1988)

The Finance Minister's office, left, is furnished with an oak desk realized by the workshops of the Mobilier National. The blinds are of white gauze netting. The wool carpet was designed by Ecart, and the standard lamp was created by Ecart Design. The armchair is covered with Edmond Petit's "Mille Points" fabric, and the floor is in grey marble with a metal grid for floor-level heating.
• The meeting area in the office of the Directeur de Cabinet, right. The ceiling light is made from a sanded metal disc and a nickel-plated cone. The meeting table is of stained and varnished oak, with a revolving bronze plate in the centre and epoxy bronze feet. The steel chairs have an epoxy bronze finish, with seats and back-rests of dark brown leather. The parquet floor is made of stained and varnished oak.

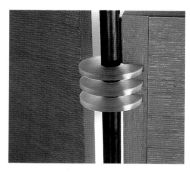

OFFICE FOR THE MINISTRY OF FINANCES

The Finance Minister's desk was designed in 1985 and exhibited at the Salon des Artistes Décorateurs in 1987. It is made of raw oak, and has drawer units, an articulated lamp and a leather writing pad. A detail of the desk drawer unit shows the discs of ground glass and the metal barrel which is connected to the desk top. • A close-up of the sofa which has an oak structure and is covered with Andrée Putman's "Chicago" fabric. • In the bathrooms, the walls and floor are covered in ceramic tiles measuring 5 x 5cm, with a frieze of mirror tiles of the same size. The fittings and wash basin are by Ecart. The luminous shelf is of glass.

OFFICE FOR A PRIVATE COMPANY, Belgium (1990)

The president's office contains a desk of black polished metal and black-stained oak with bronze details. The top is cantilevered, being supported only on one side. The integrated desk lamp is moved with the help of a small motor. • The conference table is of laminated Colorcore with bronzed metal details. At the centre is an illuminated Fresnel lens. The carpet is linen, and the Mies van der Rohe armchairs are covered in black horsehair. The door, which is 30cm thick, is made of polished metal and black-stained oak. The ceiling and walls are of polished stucco.

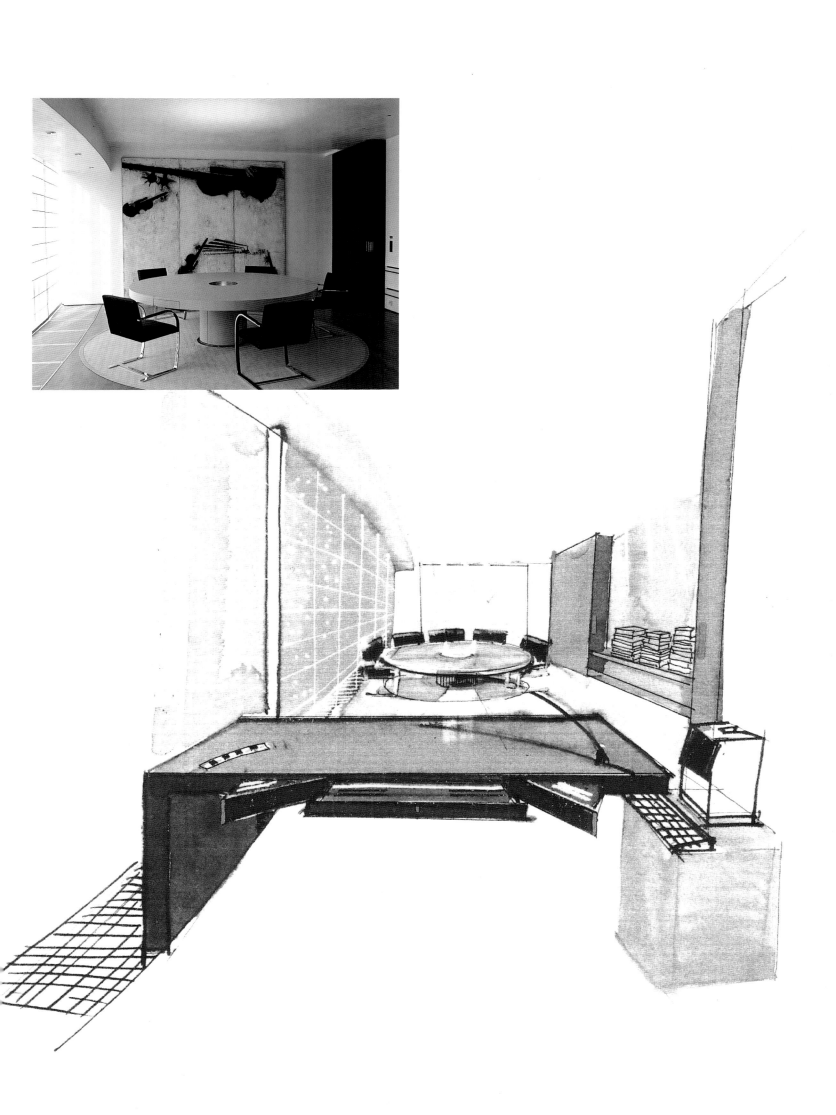

OFFICES FOR ECART,
Paris (1991)

*Detail of the office, above,
showing halogen wall lights of
lacquered white epoxy, a standing
lamp created by Ecart for the
CAPC at Bordeaux and the vertical
radiator "Acova".* • *This sliding
door, right, is of padded material
with a metal, epoxy-finished
handle. On either side of the door
are two "Techno" storage units.*
• *A detail of the banister, opposite
left, showing the decorative glass
ball.* • *The staircase, opposite
right, is made of epoxy-painted
metal. The steps are protected
with moquette. The walls and
ceiling are white matt-lacquered,
and the floor is concrete.*

OFFICES FOR ECART

The first floor of the offices have white matt-lacquered walls and ceilings, and a floor of stained and polished Lorraine boards measuring 20 by 400cm. The furniture includes a desk of stained, varnished wood by Ecart . The shelving for files is of white laminate and the notice board is of painted cork. The rug is by Andrée Putman for Toulemonde Bochart.

TOTAL,
La Défense, Paris (1994)

On the 33rd floor of one of the
towers in La Défense, Andrée
Putman and her team were
asked to design a director's
dining room and boardroom.
A place in the sky, surrounded
by space, almost too open to
light and to the dizzy heights,
the aim was to restore things
to a more domestic scale,
and to forge a link between
professional and private worlds.
For the dining room, Ecart
designed a versatile table which
could be used for an intimate
meal for two or for entertaining
32 guests. In the middle of a rug
whose cardinal points are
marked by four tall standard
lamps, a round table is set for
a select dinner party, near the
lounge area. Everywhere,
there is the subtle presence
of insubstantial materials:
mosquito netting and silk
combined in layers to filter
the dazzling light from the
windows; optical screens made
of moiré fabric stretched across
the ceiling. Small "Kraft" lamps
shed a more colourful light.
The boardroom, on the other
hand, exudes a feeling of
immateriality, with a table
made of illuminated glass,
identical treatment for all the
windows and an interplay of
light and illusive reflections.
Conducive to serious thought,
this is a minimalist, abstract
space, where all that shapes the
emptiness is light.

In the boardroom of Total's head
office in Paris, minimalism and
the interplay of reflections have
been taken to extremes. The U-
shaped illuminated boardroom
table appears to be a reflection of
the lighting. Dimmer switches
make it possible to change the
atmosphere of the room.
• The colours are derived from
the play of light on petrol: silver
for the floor, brass for the
panelling, gold for the window
fittings. The dining-room plates
are the dark greenish-blue of
petrol. The table is flanked by
four "La Lune" standard lamps,
marking the cardinal points.

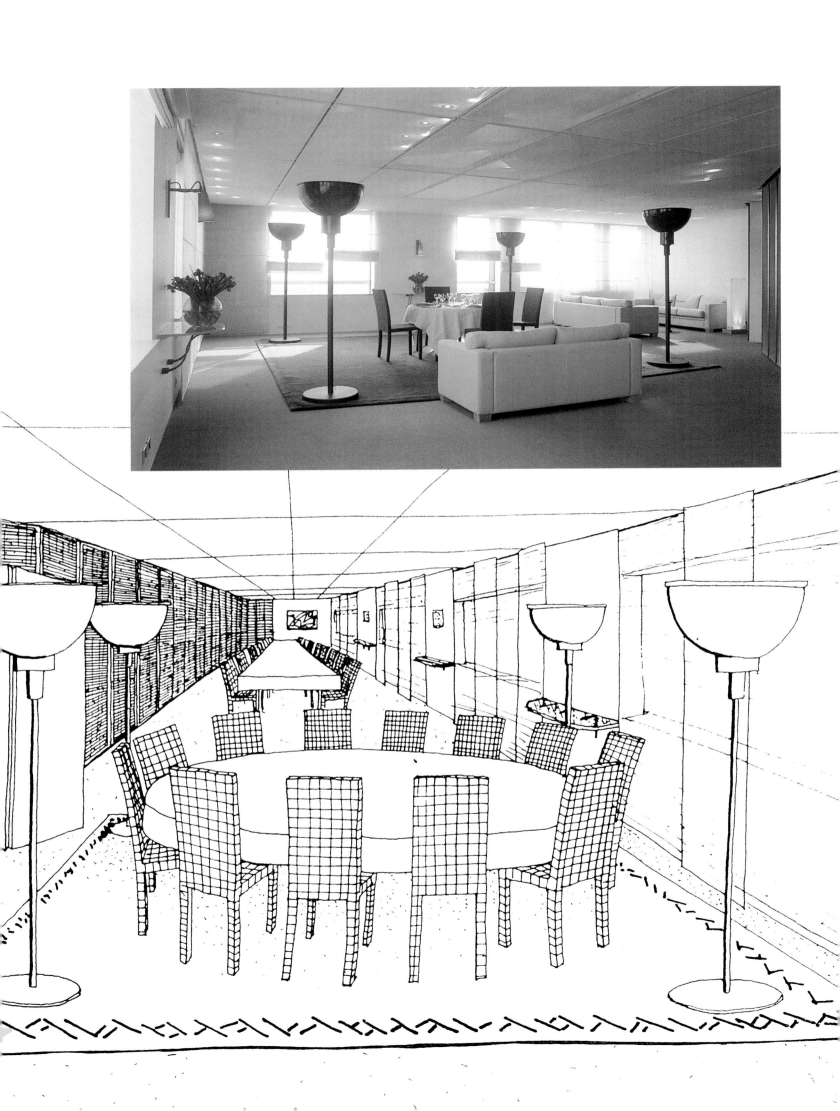

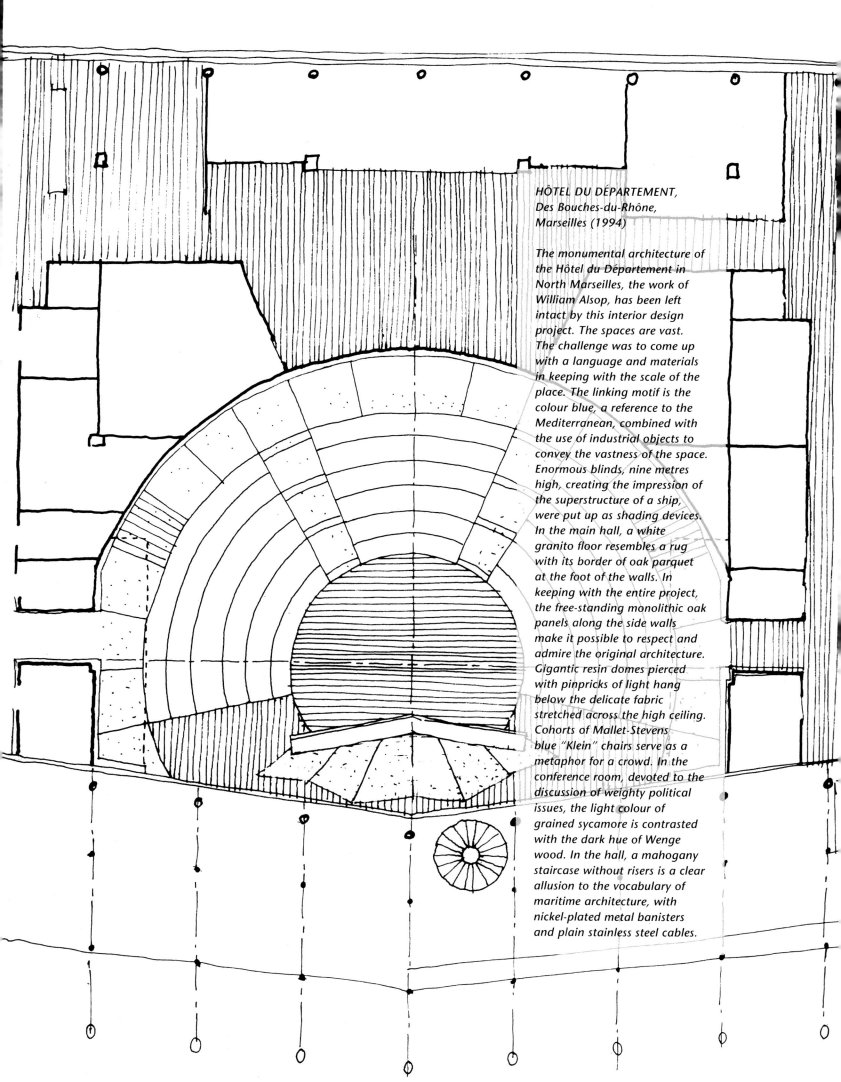

HÔTEL DU DÉPARTEMENT,
Des Bouches-du-Rhône,
Marseilles (1994)

The monumental architecture of
the Hôtel du Département in
North Marseilles, the work of
William Alsop, has been left
intact by this interior design
project. The spaces are vast.
The challenge was to come up
with a language and materials
in keeping with the scale of the
place. The linking motif is the
colour blue, a reference to the
Mediterranean, combined with
the use of industrial objects to
convey the vastness of the space.
Enormous blinds, nine metres
high, creating the impression of
the superstructure of a ship,
were put up as shading devices.
In the main hall, a white
granito floor resembles a rug
with its border of oak parquet
at the foot of the walls. In
keeping with the entire project,
the free-standing monolithic oak
panels along the side walls
make it possible to respect and
admire the original architecture.
Gigantic resin domes pierced
with pinpricks of light hang
below the delicate fabric
stretched across the high ceiling.
Cohorts of Mallet-Stevens
blue "Klein" chairs serve as a
metaphor for a crowd. In the
conference room, devoted to the
discussion of weighty political
issues, the light colour of
grained sycamore is contrasted
with the dark hue of Wenge
wood. In the hall, a mahogany
staircase without risers is a clear
allusion to the vocabulary of
maritime architecture, with
nickel-plated metal banisters
and plain stainless steel cables.

Conference room. Light entering through the tall, narrow windows is filtered by translucent boat blinds.

*Staircase in mahogany with a
stainless steel and nickel-plated
steel guardrail. The stairs are lit
by recessed spotlights.*

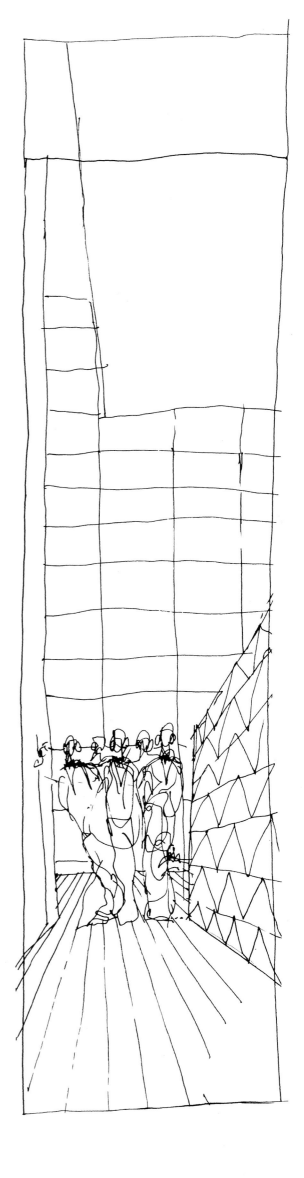

OFFICES,
Avenue Montaigne, Paris
(1993–1994)

In the lobby, an over-sized reception desk - a block of wood placed on a dais of enamelled lava - sits in the centre of a perfectly symmetrical space. On either side, wooden and meshwork cupboards set up an interplay between the visible and the invisible, offering glimpses of the colour of the files inside. Two "Paradoxe" lamps (Ecart International) complete this uncluttered geometrical layout, while boat blinds subdue the light. In the director's office, the semi-circular birchwood table goes perfectly with the light grey armchairs by Jean-Michel Frank. For displaying works of art, a glass shelf incorporated into the wooden panelling of the partitions and fitted with illuminated boxes that are deactivated when closed, creates an unbroken line running the length of the walls. This makes it possible to change the paintings which look as though they have just been propped against the honey-coloured wood. Details such as illuminated loopholes cut into the partitions, or door handles sunk into the thickness of the sliding doors, provide mysterious finishing touches to the subtle severity of these offices.

The windows are shielded by boat blinds made of mosquito netting. Furnishings include a two-seater sofa by Jean-Michel Frank, a nest of tables made of ebonized oak and "Le Compas dans l'Oeil" desk lamp (Ecart International), far left.

• A desk lamp by Mariano Fortuny sits on the desk created specially for this project, top. Paintings can be effectively displayed on an illuminated ledge running the length of the wall. In the foreground is an oil painting by Michel Haas (1993); the other oil painting is by Pierro Pizzi-Cannella (1990) (Di Meo Gallery). The light sources are contained in small metal boxes.

• The reception area, which is directly opposite the lifts, has a **soft and subdued ambience. The** sobriety of the decoration, achieved through a play of verticals (full-length lateral storage) and horizontals (3.25m reception desk and boat blinds) is discreetly emphasized by the choice of simple and elegant materials. The reception desk is made of oak, with two vertical grooves designed for the "Paradoxe" lamps.

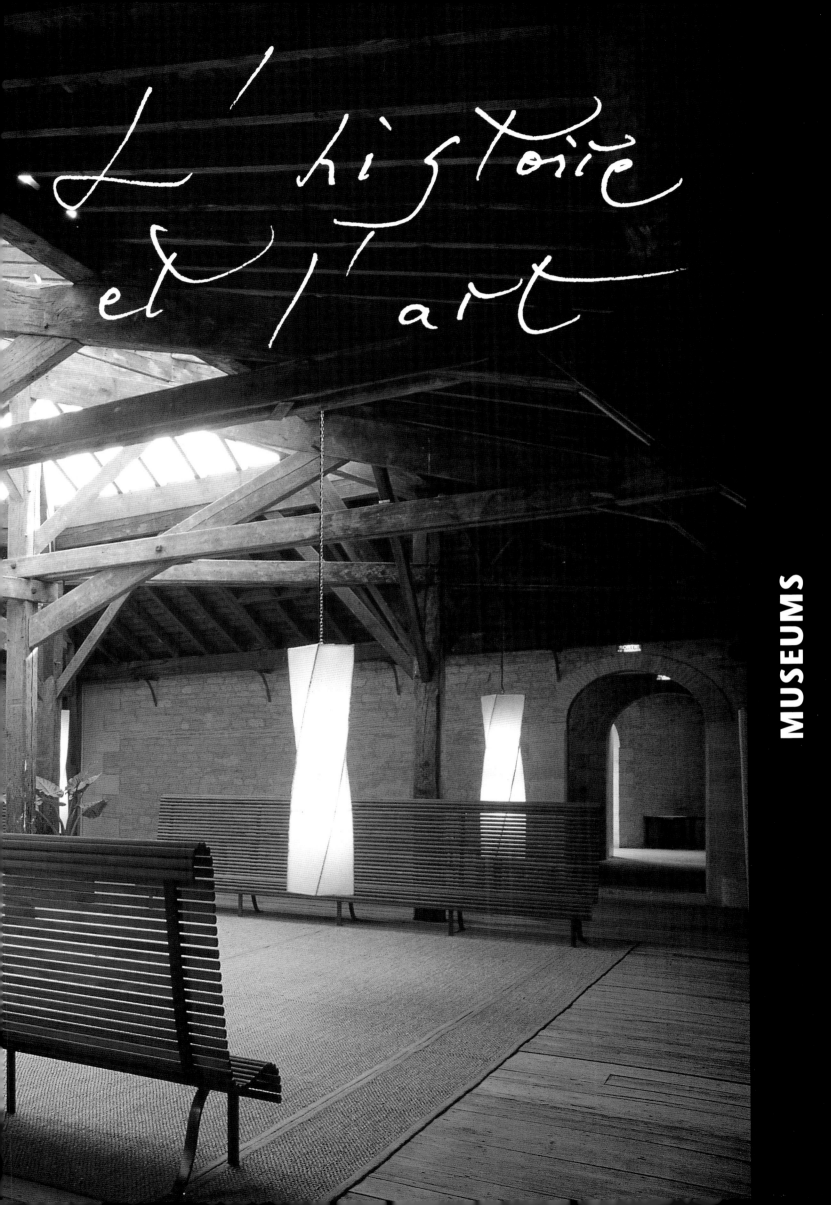

L'histoire et l'art

ART AND HISTORY

According to Andrée Putman, "in a museum, the solitude which characterises the moments spent contemplating art requires an undemanding environment. The only thing which should be considered is how to display the works to their best advantage. Our task, which covers all aspects, both major and minor, consists of different types of approach which are invisible in their various ways. This need for elimination, for self-effacement, for treading carefully, is more satisfying than it first appears: acknowledging and thereby serving those magical moments which shape you, isolate you and are at times a source of comfort."

Paradoxically, this "disappearance" is achieved by sheer hard work. How can the lighting be controlled so that it best illuminates the works without casting a reflection or being too glaring? How can the original design in an old building be rediscovered or, on the contrary, how can masses in a space devoid of interior design, where everything remains to be created, be manipulated; and, at the same time, how do you hold back, refrain from making the interior design too expressive for the intended exhibits? How do you make a decision about colour when the presence of colour is the main feature of these places? How do you tempt people to browse, to look around, to experience, guiding the route they take to communicate a reading of the works without, however, imposing this on them? Moreover, how can old buildings be modernised, incorporating technical storage areas for canvases and ensuring suitable preservation conditions, all the while bearing in mind the fact that art is there to be seen? In a museum, emptiness is no longer just a philosophy, it is the vital space needed for each work. However, the impression of disappearance which has been achieved is the opposite of neutrality; more accurately, it is the unambiguous and daring response to a feeling inspired by art. It has an affinity with timelessness, with the reconciliation of classicism and modernity, without being one or the other; it is a bold and contemporary reinterpretation.

PREVIOUS SPREAD

CAPC, Bordeaux (1984)

The atrium of the Centre d'Arts Plastiques Contemporain, in Bordeaux. The floor was made from the existing Lorraine boards. It is covered with two large sisal carpets measuring 4.80 x 9.20m. The seats are of teak with painted metal feet. The hanging lights are made from wire mesh and fire-resistant, translucent plastic film.

The CAPC, the modern art museum in Bordeaux, is in reality a place of contrasts, the result of a project which reflects two different periods. The first section of the museum, with its minimalist inspiration, true to the initial raison d'être of the warehouse, is linked to its industrial background by the use of inexpensive materials, simple, severe spaces and unitary furniture and objects - all in scale with the place which is an abstract, condensed and graphic universe. The other section of the museum, housed in some former spice warehouses in which the scent of cinnamon still lingered, inspired a different treatment, allied to the exotic nature of its earlier function. The polished veneer of the wickerwork chairs, the play of translucence and the latticework of the shutters in the Oriental style, the paper Chinese lanterns and woven mats form a sensitive, complementary and delicate language and add a touch of mellowness to the cathedral-like silence of these buildings whose proportions and high arches bring to mind images of Fontenay Abbey.

The reception area has an information desk with storage areas in laminate and epoxy metal Noir Décor. On the wall is a work by Richard Long.

CAPC

In the administration area of CAPC, left, there are laminated wood and metal desks for four people, divided by cross-shaped structures. The lamps are of opal resin and nickel-plated metal; the chairs are by Kewy. • The public toilets, right, were designed by Ecart, with wall plumbing by Biné. The wash basins are of brushed stainless steel on square pedestals made from polished concrete. To the right of each basin there is a spotlight recessed into the false ceiling. • The floors of the passages, opposite above, are lined with spotlights embedded into the smoothed concrete. Also visible here are two information stands and a row of standard lamps. • The furniture in the bookshop, opposite below, is of metal tubing and metal plate. The shelves are of laminate and are on castors. The industrial lighting is by Ecart.

MUSEE DES BEAUX ARTS, Rouen (1984)

In a historical building which has often been added to and now almost resembles some municipal building from the fifties, the paradox lies in the fact that paintings by the masters are displayed on simple plywood panels, covered in felt. Ecart's first goal was straightforward: to rediscover, under the false ceilings and behind the partitions, the original masses, outlines and glass roofs. The former mosaic parquets, dating from different eras, were replaced by a lightly-stained, highly-polished wooden floor which standardised the surfaces people walk on. White walls, a highly mathematical approach to lighting, virtually invisible blinds filtering the sunlight: everything was well thought-out to promote concentration and a meeting of emotion and art.

The glass-roofed sculpture hall, opposite. The hanging lights are of domed glass, bronzed metal and sanded glass. They are lit by halogen bulbs. The floor is terrazzo, edged with a "pointe de diamant" frieze of black and white marble. Embedded into this is a luminous gutter. The pedestals for the statues are stone. The central pool is made out of 2 x 2cm copper rocaille mosaic and stone-coloured mortar. • The museum bookshop, run by the Réunion des Musées Nationaux, has showcases in light natural oak, lit vertically and fronted with non-reflecting glass. The poster display units have bases of light oak with revolving frames and supports in brass ornamented in bronze. The posters are shown behind non-reflecting plexiglass. • The chairs are of epoxy-coated metal.

101

La quiétude et la gourmandise

TRANQUILLITY AND GOOD FOOD

Like a hotel, the restaurant is a public place which could boast the gracious atmosphere of a private place. If it were not very noisy, a little apart, with an air of discreet concern for the people who come there to take refuge from the din of the town and savour the highly distinctive pleasure of eating, it would meet the contradictory needs of being open and accessible while, within, preserving the surprise of much-needed tranquillity. But, to meet this need, a genuinely mathematical approach to space must govern the choreography of this ballet; in a place which is dedicated to peace and quiet and to the sensuality of taste, the invaluable role of the wings in a theatre is played by the sensibly placed drawers, the extra shelves and the small stopping points between tables where dishes can be prepared, facilitating the finely calculated flow of people and movements.

And the positioning of tables, their distance from each other, the quality of lighting, the regulation of what is in sight and what is concealed, the potential for withdrawing from view or, alternatively, being seen, are also part of the alchemy worked by restaurants. Their paradox lies in the fact that, while being safe havens, restful places, conducive to meetings and conversation centre-stage, there are, in the wings, two performances daily of the feverish, controlled activity which accompanies the preparation of a fine meal.

PREVIOUS SPREAD AND ABOVE

LE LAC HOTEL,
Kawaguchiko-Cho (1988)

The restaurant contains a luminous glass screen and oak tables with a central luminous glass panel. The chairs are by Michel Dufet.

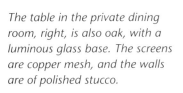

The table in the private dining room, right, is also oak, with a luminous glass base. The screens are copper mesh, and the walls are of polished stucco.

CAPC,
Bordeaux (1984)

In the restaurant of the Centre d'Art Plastique Contemporain, tables can be separated using a curved screen of metal and gauze netting which is attached to a laminate pillar. The painting is by Richard Long. • The square dining tables, measuring 90 x 90cm, are of laminate with epoxy metal Noir Décor legs on an adjustable jack. The paper lamp with a spiral of metal wire is by Kraft. The chairs are "Topacio" by Ecart. On the table there is a bunch of fragrant spices, including cinnamon as a reminder of the former function of the building.

ORCHID CLUB HOUSE,
Kobé (1992)

*In the restaurant at the Orchid
Club House, a mirror strip with
luminous panels runs around the
walls. The floor is oak parquet.
The chairs are by Michel Dufet.*

**FRENCH PAVILION, EXPO '92,
Seville (1992)**

The entry to the restaurant is
hung with a curtain of rough
linen. The walls are of varnished
scratched oak panelling, and the
flooring is of sisal. The wall
sconces were designed by Ecart.
• Inside the restaurant, the walls
are constructed of bronze Kool
Shade with recessed lights. The
screen is of steel wire mesh. The
chairs are from Andrée Putman's
"Rue du Bac" collection.

"LE BUREAU" RESTAURANT,
Monaco (1994)

The restaurant on the terrace roof of one of Monaco's most prestigious office blocks leads out into a hanging garden. Its enamelled lava floor points up the link with the outside, while the faded blue of the small tiles decorating the semi-circular bar, the stoneware and the teak are reminiscent of the materials and colours found in seaside architecture. High-backed wooden seats, covered with blue "Klein" cushions, partition the space which is punctuated by a lively array of "monte et baisse" adjustable pendant lamps hanging at different heights. Arranged back to back and joined by woven ropes resembling a fishing net, these seats conjure up the image of the spine of some huge marine animal. Slender pillars stand at intervals along this unbroken line, topped with glass balls like the ones used by fishing boats as floats. The seaside vocabulary, transferred to the top of a sky-bound Monacan building and reinterpreted by means of a deft manipulation of different dimensions, seems to imbue this completely invented place with the real, yet surreal, spirit of the nearby Mediterranean.

One of four blue-tiled waiter stations which structure the restaurant space, above.
• The central banquette seating is lit by adjustable suspension lights with parchment shades, left. The banquettes are made of teak slats, reminiscent of garden furniture, with denim-covered cushions. The banquette supports contain a curved, bevelled-edge mirror, typical of Parisian brasseries, and the structure is topped by glass balls.

L'illusion et

l'apparence

ILLUSION AND APPEARANCE

These are mainly fashion shops, often designers' shops, and are central to a certain idea of elegance, of appearance and show, of the play of reflections and images. Often changing, ephemeral, these shops are like a snapshot which captures a season's fleeting look. Being most closely connected with the body, clothes in western mythology comply with a sort of immediacy, a transitory impression akin to a theatrical performance whose transient nature does not detract from its dramatic qualities. A shop would therefore be the *mise en scène* of those accessories necessary for a performance which is rehearsed here, in front of the mirrors, with the often anxious interrogation of the image reflected back by the silvered surface: the drama of youth, of beauty, of time, all faithfully and uncompromisingly monitored by clothes.

The interior design and décor of these places meet different needs every time, just as a text can be interpreted in many different ways. The scenography may be inspired by a minimalist, refined vision in which an article of clothing would be presented like a short-lived production; it may also be that something fictional has to be designed due to constraints of space - for example, a staircase hewn from golden rock... unless the theme of childhood generates a mood of playfulness, flippancy and entertainment.

PREVIOUS SPREAD

SALON FOR AZZEDINE ALAIA,
Paris (1985)

A detail of the mirrored wall of the fitting rooms.

This project - the couturier's first salon - combined several elements. First, it was a matter of designing a shop on the ground floor of what was to be a house, and a workshop. Secondly, it was necessary to carry on the idea of a retail outlet in the form of an apartment, which had once again been taken up by Azzedine Alaïa, who used to organise his fashion parades at home, in the rue de Bellechasse. In this particular town house in the Marais district, Ecart's approach was initially to define four masses, one per level. In the shop, the subtle simplicity of the project is summed up by a gleaming black marble floor, panelling on the walls enclosing storage spaces, and clothes lining two other walls. Two things intrude on this empty space. Cloth fitting rooms are concealed by a folding three-sided, mirrored screen. This unit, an object in its own right, floating on the black lake of the floor, represents in itself a view of fashion and its illusions. On the other side of the room, there is a huge mirror which seems fixed to the floor. It spreads out its side display units in which a shoe, presented like a piece of jewellery, becomes something out of the ordinary.

The interior of the salon showing the walls and ceiling of grey stucco and the black marble floor. The walls of the fitting rooms are made up of nets and folding mirrors with nickel hinges. The wall light by Ruhlmann was reissued by Ecart. The chair is by Mallet-Stevens. • Detail of a swivelling accessory cupboard in black lacquer showing the "corner pivot" hinge mechanism.

115

**SHOP FOR THIERRY MUGLER,
Paris (1978)**

*The staircase in the Thierry
Mugler shop in place des Victoires
is surrounded by "rocks" of
moulded fibreglass and decorated
with Italian gold mosaic. • The
walls and furniture are of
Vetricolor tiling, the rock is made
of resin and sand and the
luminous ceiling is of metal and
glass.*

SHOP FOR EBEL,
London (1987)

The shop has an illuminated metal cornice in sage green which matches the vicuña wool carpet. It is furnished with chairs and armchairs with horsehair seats and semi-circular tables with pivoting drawers. The lights are made of nickel-plating and ground glass and can be moved up and down mechanically.

SHOP FOR EBEL,
New York (1989)

The entrance is constructed of
Cremo Marfill stone, with a
surround and door of glass and
black metal.

119

This hairdressing and beauty salon on the rue du Faubourg St Honoré became a space filled with light and water, dedicated to beauty and feelings of well-being. Tiled with mosaic throughout, showered by light, the spaces at Carita promote function and comfort, in a universe akin to that of the Roman baths, but with the latest in modern technological equipment and the Parisian concept of discreet luxury.

The reception area, far left. The desk is of limed oak with a rim and skirt of pink and grey tesserae. The stairs are of wood and metal; the floor is of Carrara marble. The glass doors in the background contain bubbles which give the effect of water.
• A doorway of steel blue Savoie marble with bronze studs, centre, leads to the men's salon. The central unit is tessellated with laminated wood sections. • Close-up of a basin made from vitrified cement. The tessellated base has a rim of stainless steel.

SALON FOR BALENCIAGA, Paris (1989)

A dress-making theme characterises the fitting rooms of the Balenciaga salon in avenue George V. The curtains of pattern cutter's cloth are tied back with red braid. The flooring consists of riveted pieces of stage canvas. The stool has corroded metal legs and a piped red velvet seat.
• Accessories are displayed in red velvet-lined compartments inside a cabin trunk. The doors of the trunk are edged with a strip of corroded metal. The sham black leather covering is decorated with round-headed brass nails.
• A detail of the cabin trunk, showing the red tassels bound with gold which serve as handles.

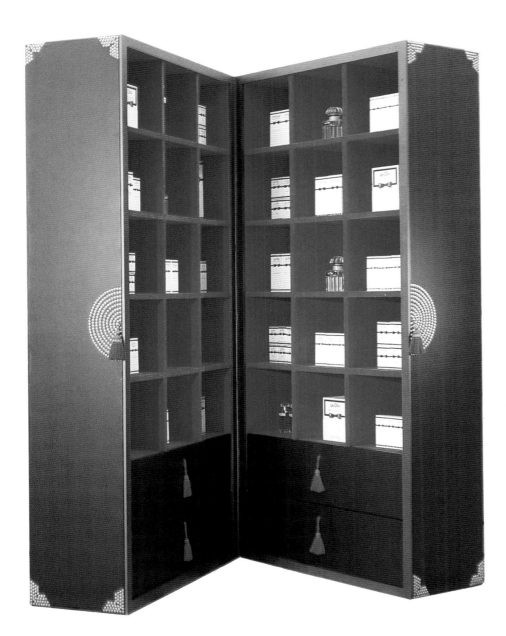

MAN WOMAN SHOP,
Manchester (1991)

*This project - a menswear shop -
was carried out with limited
resources and represents another
aspect of fashion, based on a
dramatic look at transience. In
contrast to the bare concrete
floor, screens tiled with mosaic,
which begin halfway down the
wall and extend to the floor,
indicate the spaces where the
display shelves are fixed to the
concrete walls. In order to order
the space, creating display units
and fitting rooms, simple fabric
panels modify and structure a
rectangular mass. Lighting is
provided by illuminated paper
columns which pick out the
points of light concealed in the
shelves.*

*The view towards the entry. The
walls and central stand are of
polished cement, and the display
area consists of glass mosaic tiles.
The hanging lights are made of
stretched Mylar, wire mesh and a
steel frame. The mannequins were
made by Pucci to Andrée
Putman's design.*

SHOP FOR GEORGES RECH,
London (1991)

*The ground floor has an
enamelled lava floor, painted
walls and a staff ceiling. The
seven display cases for accessories
around the edge of the stairwell
are made of glass with a nickel-
plated metal frame and feet of
blue scratched oak. • A view of
the basement. The stairs are
made of enamelled lava, covered
with a sand-coloured tufted wool
carpet. A screen made from
doubled gauze netting descends
from the ground floor. Around the
edge of the stairwell there are four
display cases. On the floor in front
of the fitting rooms there is a
semi-circular tufted wool rug. The
armchairs are of fabric by Casal
and flannel, with feet of nickel-
plated metal and blue scratched
oak.*

SHOP FOR CACHAREL,
Barcelona (1992)

For the first Cacharel Enfants
boutique, Ecart immediately
adopted a scale commensurate
with childhood: everything
within arm's reach and at eye-
level for a child. The boutique
toys with fairground variations:
a huge straw hat with its lucky
dip, and furniture which
playfully alludes to bunk beds
and swings, with ropes and nets
which shape a flexible,
transitory space fit for playing
games - a simple, cheerful
universe which is devoid of false
luxury and is extremely
undemanding.

The shop is furnished with
modular units made up of white-
painted wood shelves on a
structure of white resin rope,
above. The display cases are also
on a rope structure with a base of
netting. The fitting rooms are
circular cubicles made of fabric.
• Sketch of a circular cubicle,
right. • The double-sided mirror
on castors, far right, is framed
with white resin rope.

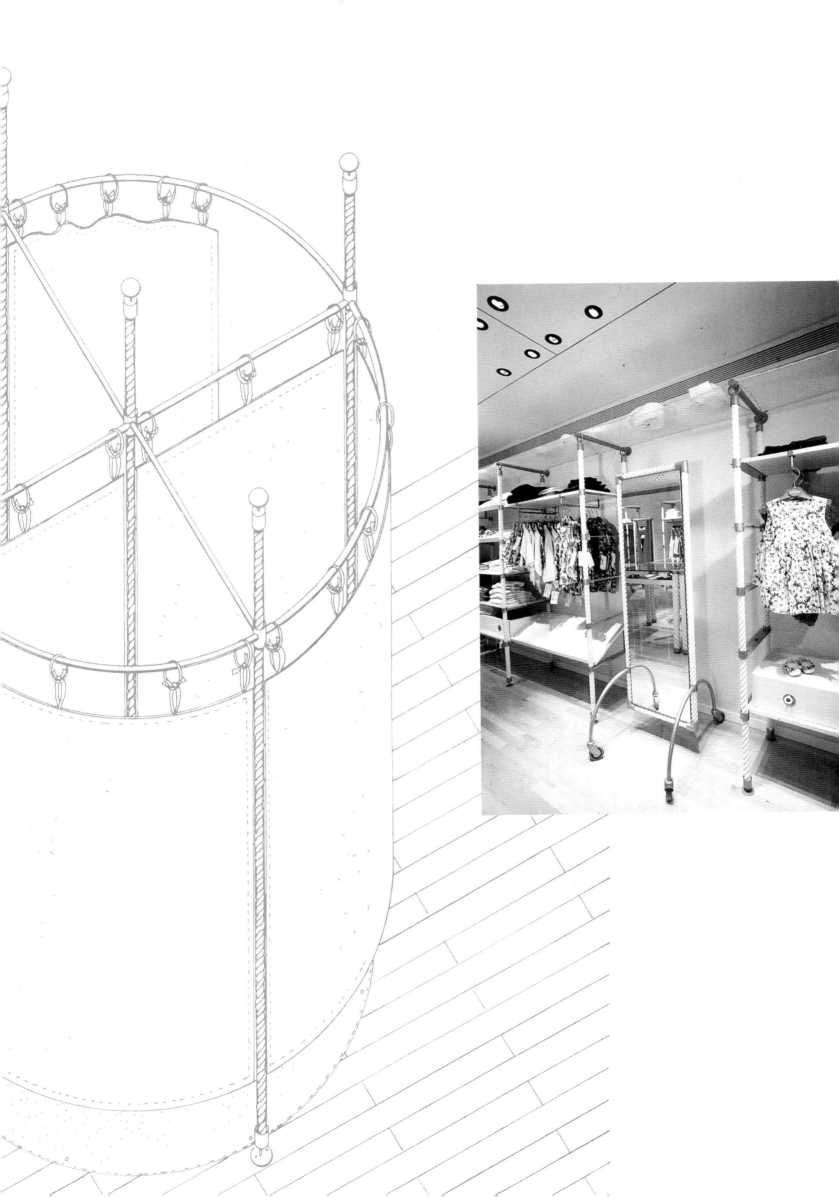

CONNOLLY,
London (1995)

One of the most prestigious saddlers has set up shop in these former stables, renowned throughout nineteenth-century London, to sell products connected with sport, including riding, hunting and motor-racing. Ecart has preserved the spirit of the place by retaining the former stalls and by paving the floor with small 5x5cm stone flags of the sort found on the old floors of traditional stables. A huge saddler's table found in the factory is used for display purposes, while another table, called the "Elephant Table", showcases all kinds of precious accessories in its small horizontal display cases. The inverted "bowls" of the tall standard lamps provide soft lighting, as at the CAPC in Bordeaux. Another treasure unearthed at the factory is a cupboard once used for storing samples. This has a hundred labelled drawers, one of which is marked "empty", and helps to link the modernity of the site to time-honoured traditions of craftsmanship. Creating a contrast between a sort of "Arte Povera" and the luxury of the products on sale, the Connolly shop flirts with modesty in a spirit of subtle irony which bears certain similarities to Jane Austen's fiction.

At the centre of the Connolly shop is the "Elephant Table" in bleached oak, left. Over 5m long, the table also serves as a display surface. Two glass display cases are built into the table ends.
• The original staircase has been refurbished, above left, and leads to offices. "La Lune" standard lamps have been transformed into suspension lights and provide a soft ambient light in this area.

The owner of these shops on the Rue Royale shares Andrée Putman's passion for thirties furniture, and Ecart wanted to achieve the most uncluttered, most unobtrusive embodiment of the art of "wiping the slate clean" which is the product of a skilful manipulation of space. As a result, light is the governing idea of this project, as seen in the concept of a "cushion of light" due to which all the furniture seems to float several centimetres above the floor. This impression of magic at work is sustained by the glass shelves which resemble wafers of light, and by the niches which appear to have been contrived randomly and asymmetrically in the partitions and birch-wood panelling lining the walls. In these niches, accessories, illuminated like one-off designs, assume the quality of rare or slightly comical objects. A huge spiral staircase forms a metal helix, paring down space even further until it appears to be a coil of energy creating three-dimensional or over-hanging effects from one level to another.

An immense spiral staircase with a metal guardrail, above left, leads to a vast basement. An overall effect of brightness has been created without the use of conspicuous lighting. • In the basement of this huge shop, the parquet flooring is made of light wood, left. An illuminated plinth at floor level relieves the strict layout of the cupboards and shelves. • The asymmetrical niches designed for accessories are also used as cupboards, below.

BALLY,
Zurich, Cologne and Geneva
(1993)

Andrée Putman's starting point for the creation of Bally's international image was a single idea: that of the staircase, the only time shoes appear in movement. This idea of the staircase also became the image of men and women walking, of movement, of the desire to reach a destination. The product became an object in its own right and is viewed as such. The window displays effect a transition between the street and the shop by means of several stairs, which are featured again inside the shop. Each "object" is illuminated, explicit, invaluable. The central motif becomes a spiral, a small tower shaped like a snail shell around which customers can walk, and this motif is picked up by the central ceiling light. The guardrail of the staircase in its turn is also used to promote this display which focuses so minutely on detail. There is wry humour in the treatment of a small footstool and the small Bally chairs, covered in greyish-brown cotton fabric, which are laced up like shoes. Wooden floors, curtains in heavy fabric for the fitting rooms where customers can try on their range of clothes, mirrors, and delicate mesh details combined with light wood, create an understated, friendly and attentive atmosphere. A huge cabin trunk contains outfits and accessories and, in some shops - the height of sophistication and style - shoes are placed in small boxes which appear between the two thicknesses of glass forming the street door.

Bally, Zurich. Niches in the walls contain a display of period shoes, which can be viewed from the escalators, above left. • Bally, Geneva. A guardrail designed as an illuminated staircase made of sand-blasted glass makes it possible to display shoes all the way up the staircase, above. • Bally, Cologne. The seats covered in beige fabric make a veiled reference to lace-up shoes, above right. Shoes can be seen at their best on staircases. This is the prevailing theme of the concept which, starting with the shop windows, is used to display the shoes. • The delicate pink resin ceiling light mirrors the spiral shoe display stand, right. This is made of satin-finished walnut on top of a mesh and mosquito netting structure. Cabin trunks are used to display clothes and accessories.

L'emotion
le silence

EMOTION AND SILENCE

A gallery is rather like a temple of art. It must inspire respect but also tempt the visitor to follow the visual progression of works on display and for sale. In this sense, it is a cross between a

museum, given its cultural orientation, and a shop, given its economic and urban position. Its silence is taken from the museum and, from the shop, it derives the importance of opening on to the street and being accessible to the passer-by. This contradictory state of affairs compels the interior designer to work a skilful alchemy on space. A priori, devoid of any "décor", the gallery is an empty space structured by masses which compose it and proportions which guide the eye. Since its function is to house works which are radically different by nature, it must be a sort of organised "blank page", waiting to be written on. The gallery must give the impression, both in terms of the visitor and the works, that it has been designed specifically for whatever is on display. It has therefore even more opportunity than a museum to practise the art of elimination, of fine detail. Materials and lighting become a very unobtrusive and refined type of embellishment. This is the sort of ambition nurtured by architecture: to achieve a space which echoes with its own silence, rather like a place of spiritual devotion, allowing emotions to run free in the contemplation of art.

PREVIOUS SPREAD

PUTMAN FROMENT GALLERY,
Paris (1989)

Detail of the sliding door at the gallery, showing the white epoxy metal frame, opal Stadip glass and nickel-plated grip.

Detail showing lightwells, far left.
• A luminous slit in the wall, left.
• Detail of the glass roof, below,
which is made of painted metal
and wired glass.

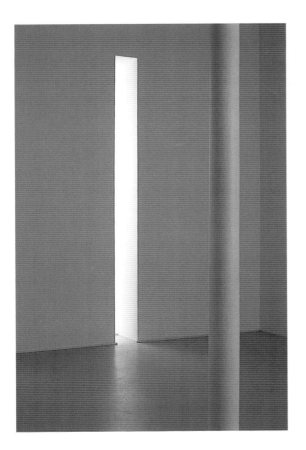

ISY BRACHOT GALLERY,
Paris (1991)

This project was to convert the ground floor and basement of a building into an art gallery, in rue Guénégaud, the area in Paris where all the galleries are situated. The first step was to accomplish "the awareness of a mass", by eliminating the partitions and creating an empty, silent space, full of promise, with wide wooden boards on the floor recalling the deck of a ship. The facade is divided into irregular parallelepipeds, of which one - the door - is opaque, surrounded by the others which are transparent. The curve of the arch, at the back of the gallery, indicates the more baroque space of the basement, reached by a small minimalist stairway which has a refined design.

The facade of the gallery, showing ironwork and the solid door of bronze-coloured corroded metal, left. • Detail of the main door, above. The door handle is made of nickeled metal tube and transparent glass. • The director's office, right, has a brushed oak desk. The armchairs are by Andrée Putman for De Sede, and the carpet is sisal with a linen border. The floor is of varnished concrete.

LEE,
Paris (1994)

In a street in the Saint Germain quarter of Paris, Ecart has fitted out a small gallery and apartment. The challenge of this project was to establish a link between the different sections of a complicated layout and, more importantly, to find ways of manipulating an extremely small area. The different levels are reached by retractable staircases which make it possible to free up the space or completely alter its function. The precision and craftsmanship of their design make these staircases objects in their own right, functional elements of a style of décor inspired by ships. On the first floor, in full view of the ground floor, a guardrail made of a double thickness of glass is used as a raised display case. On the floors, the transitions from light wood to stoneware serve to demarcate the space, while a row of doorways extending from floor to ceiling creates an illusory perspective. Although completely abstract in concept, this project conceals various structural details - such as a wall with a cut-off corner which shapes the space - or secrets - such as the box in the wall which opens to reveal a small writing table. This brings to mind the meticulous details of ships' cabins where cramped space and movement call for mechanisms of the utmost precision.

The metal hydraulic staircase leading from the ground floor of the gallery, left. The pilaster to the left conceals all the technical services. At the top of the staircase are display-case guardrails and a stair leading to the second-floor apartment. The gallery floor is made of tinted and waxed concrete. • From the first floor of the gallery, above, can be seen the hydraulic staircase that can be raised or lowered to provide access or isolate the ground floor. The display case in glass and nickel-plated brass also acts as a guardrail. To the right is an electric stairway, also in metal, which gives access to a private apartment on the second floor. • Detail of a recessed wall sconce in the second-floor apartment. The light source is recessed into the wall, and luminosity is increased through a vertical sand-blasted glass element which protrudes from the nickel-plated brass frame to light the passageway. • On the ground floor of the gallery is a small writing table, 1ft square, which can be folded into the wall when not in use. The light emanating from the niche is activated when the table is pulled down.

141

Visage
et paysage

APPEARANCE AND LANDSCAPE

The design and décor of an apartment reflect above all an awareness and understanding of a person, the realisation of a unique relationship. That is why, as Andrée Putman often says, "it is only possible to design an apartment for a close friend." This does not mean doing their portraits, however, which would immediately be an interpretation of them; it is more a case of assisting them to create their own self-portraits, a task which requires a lucid and perceptive approach. Of course, it also means giving them the benefit of the widest experience possible regarding allocation of space, choice of materials and remembering details which have to be thought out to be forgotten, so as to make life easier. "We merely manipulate space and functions, then everything is shifted around for several months and, a year after we have finished, a home becomes truly beautiful because it has succeeded in winning the difficult bet of becoming totally autonomous, a living entity."

PREVIOUS SPREAD

METROPOLITAN TOWER,
New York (1985)

Detail of the bedroom in the model apartment. The table lamp is by Félix Aublet.

A corner bedroom in the model apartment. The furniture includes a Pierre Chareau table, a winged chair by Patrick Naggar and a mirror by Eileen Gray.
• The entrance to the apartment. The walls and ceiling are panelled with sycamore.

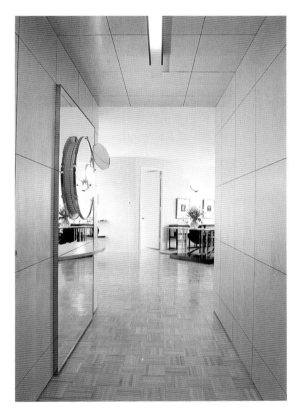

ANDREE PUTMAN'S APARTMENT, Paris (1979)

Four columns hung with lengths of gauze netting separate off the bedroom. A large ink drawing by P. Alechinsky has been leant against one of the columns. Under the window there is a sixties "Brion Vega" stereo system. The furniture includes a shell-shaped seat and an eighteenth-century German grandfather clock with mirror-glass casing engraved with a pattern of vines. The two black lacquer tables decorated with ivory were designed in about 1930 for Jeanne Lanvin's colleague Drian. The lamp in the foreground is by Serge Manzon.

ANDRÉE PUTMAN'S APARTMENT, Paris (1994)

On the kitchen wall, above a long table made of enamelled lava, hangs a collection of letters, signed drawings or keepsakes from artist friends. Around the table are "Kohn" bentwood chairs and bench. • In the bathroom, a wide, tiled counter accommodates the wash basin which is actually a small washing-up sink. On the left, a lamp with a streaked glass shade hangs from the ceiling by a chain. The bath is a continuation of the tiled counter. Wickerwork drawers in niches store everything usually hidden in cupboards. One of the window panes is made of blue glass.

The main room, far left, with a
chaise longue by Le Corbusier
next to the bedroom. On the wall
to the left of the tree is a painting
by Bram van Velde. In the
foreground is the table by Drian,
Jeanne Lanvin's collaborator.
• The main change to the loft
since 1978 is the removal of the
wall in front of the landing. The
extensive terrace is now reached
by means of a glass partition, left.
• The terrace, below, with a
weathervane by Roland Roure,
"Le mangeur de libellules", and
chaises longues by Robert Mallet-
Stevens. The kitchen is in the
greenhouse.

MAIME ARNODIN AND DENISE FAYOLLE'S APARTMENT, Paris (1980)

The white-tiled bathroom; the wash basin is of chromed metal and Carrara marble.

JAMES BROWN'S APARTMENT,
Paris (1992)

*The bathroom in James Brown's
apartment is realized
entirely in grey ceramic tiles
measuring 5 x 5cm. Around the
walls there is a frieze of blown
and gilded glass. Cupboard space
is concealed behind the bevelled
mirror. A light made of sanded
glass is set into the ceiling, and
Chinese lanterns provide ambient
lighting.*

151

**STAN LEVY AND COLETTE BEL'S
APARTMENT,
Paris (1981)**

*The library, above. The furniture is
by OUD. • The apartment is
furnished with fifties chairs and
has a terrazzo floor. The Eileen
Gray rug was reissued by Ecart
International.*

APARTMENT,
Paris (1982)

The office in a Paris apartment. The bookshelves and work table are of dark brown laminated wood and epoxy-resin-coated metal. The work table includes a tilting writing desk. The table has a ground-glass top and a metal base which is on castors. The floor is covered with a grey tufted carpet.

KARL LAGERFELD'S APARTMENT, Rome (1982)

The bedroom of Karl Lagerfeld's apartment, left. The chequered top of the pedestal table is of ebony and citron wood. • In the bathroom, below, the walls are covered with black and white ceramic tiles. The "Satellite" mirror by Eileen Gray was reissued by Ecart International (see page 172).

**KARL LAGERFELD'S STUDIO,
Paris (1993)**

*Karl Lagerfeld's studio in Paris is
dominated by an extremely large
round wooden table (2.8m in
diameter) with a rotating central
turntable. This work surface is
also ideal for improvised meals.
The walls are covered with recent
photographs by Karl Lagerfeld.
Above the "Lazy Susan" table
hangs a large "monte et baisse"
adjustable ceiling light with a
galvanised iron shade and
Baccarat crystal pendants.*

PRIVATE VILLA,
Belgium (1992)

One of the children's bathrooms in this family home contains a bath standing on four marble balls. On the right, a bentwood cupboard prefigures a band of white tiling designed to look like foam on the wave described by the blue floor. • Detail of the 2x2cm glass mosaic tiles, right, which draw attention to the cupboard doors and protect the wood.

TAUBMAN APARTMENT,
Detroit (1984)

In the bathroom of Mr and Mrs Taubman's apartment, the wash basin is set into a tiled unit which has white lacquered doors and drawers with handles by Gaudí. The parquet floor is of Carrara marble. The towel rail is made up of a glass bar resting on two nickel-plated tubes. The room is lit by a luminous panel of sanded glass set into the wall, above.
• The bath is set into bolted marble and is surrounded by walls of glass. A tiled luminous cornice lights up a curved ceiling covered in glass squares measuring 2 x 2cm. Visible in the foreground is a dividing door of sanded glass with a frame and handle of nickel-plated brass.

DIDIER GRUMBACH'S APARTMENT, Paris (1986)

The dining room. The floor is stained and varnished parquet, and the walls are matt-lacquered. The dining table is made of epoxy lacquered metal and sanded varnished glass. Visible in the background is the kitchen which is tiled in grey stoneware tiles measuring 5 x 5cm. Sliding wired-glass doors with nickel-plated brass frames separate the two rooms.

HUNT RESIDENCE,
San Francisco (1982)

The staircase in the Hunt residence
has metal banisters decorated with a
glass ball. The steps are parquet, the
walls are painted and the ceilings of
staff. As well as the central nickel-
plated brass reflector, there is
lighting in the cornices.

ROSENBERG APARTMENT,
New York (1986)

The glass-roofed terrace, right, with its boat blinds and floor of grey ceramic tiles. • The wash basin in the bathroom, far right, is of grey oak with a white enamel bowl and black granite top. The walls and floor are of pâté de verre. The recessed wall lights are of sanded glass and nickel-plated metal.

MICHEL GUY'S APARTMENT,
Paris (1983)

In the drawing room the floor has been stained black and is carpeted with Eileen Gray's "Black Magic" rug. • The bathroom floor is of Carrara marble, and the ball feet of the bath are painted to imitate marble. The nickel taps are by Juif Delepine.

CHRISTOPH VON WEYHE'S APARTMENT,
Paris (1988)

The living room has matt-lacquered painted staff walls and a stained and varnished oak floor, below. The staircase is of lacquered epoxy metal, and the front of the kitchen is of epoxy metal and wired glass. • The guardrail around the mezzanine, right, is made of glass and epoxy. • The bathroom walls are tiled and patterned with a frieze of 2 x 2cm squares, far right. Storage space is concealed behind the mirror. Other fittings include a luminous sanded-glass shelf and recessed wall lights.

JEAN-PAUL GOUDE'S HOUSE, Paris (1992)

When describing this project, Andrée Putman began with her treatment of the bathroom, which is not surprising, because contrary to prevailing opinion, she believes that the bathroom is one of the most important rooms in the home. Her decision in 1967, when designing Maïmé Arnodin's apartment, to devote three windows and the largest area to the bathroom, while the bedroom was simply a small, peaceful monastic space, already betokened this idea of a place where inwardness and intimacy revelled in broad daylight and where the body, both physically and figuratively, had room to breathe. She then, as is the case here, chose the most unremarkable 10x10cm white ceramic tiles for the floor and the walls. "In this delightful small home where Virginia creeper resembles lettuce leaves trembling at the first breath of wind and framing the windows with a border of foliage", the bathroom is an exercise in discipline, since everything can be seen and none of the fixtures provides any excuse for a disappearing act. All the accessories are visible on the shelves, the tiled floor and surfaces become masses and shapes, the bath and the two washbasins become objects in their own right. The bathroom, a variation on this unassuming and unremarkable theme, is also square, and this tactic, taken to its extreme, becomes the distillation of a space fashioned from the geometrical repetition of a simple shape.

Next door, the bedroom continues this idea of taking a simple, severe element to its logical conclusion, the central character being the bed, whose four uprights become columns which appear to support the ceiling. Here, however, the tactic has been inverted and the columns are storage areas which form the motif of a totem pole, freeing up the walls and guarding their secrets.

In the dining room, a large white-tiled table set against the mahogany panels echoes the stark contrasts between the colours, dazzlingly bright and dissolving into shadow, which interact with the light and the foliage.

The bathroom is tiled white, creating a variety of visual effects and convenient features, left. A large storage area under the shelf is partially obscured by small, square walls placed directly below the mirrors. To the right is the access to the bath, which is also tiled, and shelves. • In the Wenge wood bedroom, top right, the square columns of the bed contain invisible cupboards.
• The dining room is furnished with a tiled stone table and silver Mallet-Stevens chairs. The lush foliage at the tall, narrow windows softens all these straight lines.

FANTASY AND ACTUALITY

An interior design project draws its energy from the clash between décor and reality. Andrée Putman's work takes this paradox to its farthest extreme. Dreams and stories are the tools she uses with penetrating insight to manipulate the uncompromising reality of space and the strict mathematics of measurement. Her meeting with Peter Greenaway gave her the opportunity to create an imaginary world in which meaning reigned supreme. The narrative, poetic and metaphorical function of the place was all that mattered. Its *raison d'être* was to express the soul of the central character and her mystery. And although Andrée Putman has always practised the art of what she calls "wiping the slate clean", which involves creating places specifically for their future role and, therefore, working with a certain degree of freedom, in this film, her intuitions, choices, manipulation of scale, incongruity, humour and abstraction, as well as her passion for materials, found their ultimate form of expression. Each of these qualities was carried towards the "infinitude" of fiction and yet kept tightly under control.

The kitchen, shown left, in the sketch and on the previous spread, is carved out of a block of stone. This is a homage to the gardens of Katsuura and a reference to Nagiko's origins. A huge cluster of cooking implements hangs above the work surface. • The spine-like illuminated path leading to the bedroom belonging to Nagiko (the heroine of the film) starts in front of the front door made of printed aluminium, below. This path provides access to all the living areas of the apartment. A forest of bamboo stands on either side of the door. • The bath, bottom, stands on four feet on an island of paving stones in the middle of a gravelled floor, like a Western object set down in a Zen garden.

"THE PILLOW BOOK",
(1995)

This is the story of a young girl in the eleventh century whose father lovingly paints birthday greetings on his child's cheeks in exquisite calligraphy. She is reborn ten centuries later as a top international model, obsessed by this memory, and constantly searching for lover-calligraphers. What style of décor would suit her? What would her home be like? Andrée Putman has created an apartment which combines tradition and futurism, positing one view of the future. The distillation of space, an inhabited void, introduces a reference to Asian culture. Huge lengths of bamboo represent a Zen forest, evoking the spirit of stone gardens. And the purpose of each room is defined by the object situated at its centre, like the face of a Narcissus contemplating himself in the mirror.

Objets

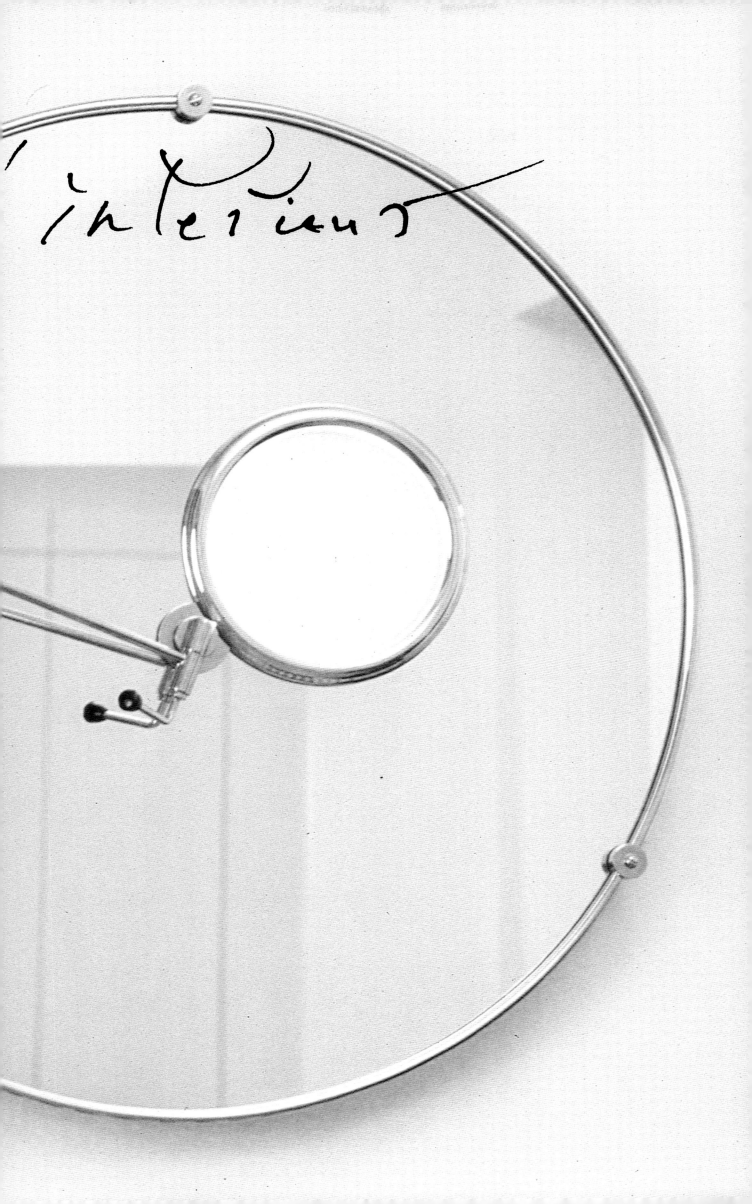

intérieur

HOUSEHOLD OBJECTS

Ecart's story began with several pieces of furniture by some of the leading architects in the modern movement, firstly with prototypes built from designs, then "re-editions", which enabled the general public, for whom these objects were initially intended ("beautiful things for everyone", the aim of the Bauhaus), to rediscover an entire period of design history devoted to the sole passion of a very few experts. Ecart, carrying on its "archaeology into modern times" by adding to its catalogue, has, at the same time and in line with a very consistent policy, been issuing the work of many young contemporary designers, like Sacha Ketoff, Olivier Gagnère, Patrick Naggar, Lachevski, Sylvain Dubuisson, etc. Furthermore, the drawing office has been pursuing two types of activity since it was set up. On the one hand, it handles furniture design for specific projects. It is unusual for Ecart not to design the furniture for a space it is working on; this always provides a fresh opportunity for designing new forms and re-interpreting functions. These designs are occasionally issued by Ecart themselves as an independent line. On the other hand, the drawing office does design work for other manufacturers, like De Sede or Mobilier National, who commission Andrée Putman to produce furniture collections bearing the Ecart label. This branch of activity within Ecart is closely bound up with a certain belief about the character of a place, a belief which claims that each space is so distinctive that everything must be designed, while one or other of these objects, the product of specific circumstances, may in time become part of mainstream contemporary design.

Eileen Gray began designing carpets as early as 1910, though she produced most between 1923 and 1930. This re-edition of her "Mediterranean" rug is hand-tufted (60,000 tufts/m²) with a pile height of 18mm. • A re-edition of Eileen Gray's "Transat" chair (1927) in beechwood, chrome plating and leather. Height: 79cm max. Width: 55cm Depth: 106cm

PREVIOUS SPREAD

Eileen Gray's "Satellite" mirror (1927) has a nickel-plated brass structure. The sanded convex glass shade takes two 15W light bulbs. The magnifying mirror is adjustable. Height: 73cm Width: 90cm Depth: 17cm.

175

Ecart's "Rue des Minimes" collection (1993), far left, comprising a chair, armchair and bench in beech with a lacquer finish. • Left, a cupboard by Pierre Chareau (c. 1928), "Lune" floor lamps (1989), "Léger Regel" coffee table by Paul Mathieu and Michael Ray, and an "Ecriture" rug. • Félix Aublet's desk lamp (1925), below left. This has nickel-plated brass spherical elements. The lower sphere contains a cast-iron ballast. The base and prongs are of nickel-plated zinc alloy. Height: 42cm, 32cm Diameter: 18cm 12cm • An armchair designed for the "Le Lac" hotel (1991-92), top right. The frame is wooden with Bultex foam upholstery covered with fabric or leather. The feet are of lacquered steel tube, attached by nickel-plated fixtures. Height: 80cm Width: 77cm Depth: 75cm • Robert Mallet-Stevens' armchair (1927-28), above right, has a structure in lacquered steel tube and sheet steel, and foam cushions. Height: 73cm Width: 67cm • The table, right, was created by Jacques-Henri Lartigue for his own use in 1918. The spherical element is of synthetic resin, the top and base of high-lustre black and white lacquered redwood. It has been re-issued in a limited signed edition of 100. Height: 75cm Width: 196cm Depth: 120cm

• A table created by Jean-Michel Frank and Adolphe Chanaux for Jean-Pierre Guerlain (c.1935), right. The top is veneered oak and the sides of the top and the legs are of brushed oak with a natural varnished finish. Height: 75cm Width: 220cm Depth: 118cm

Ecart Design's "La Lune" writing desk (1990), left, has a wood cover and top and is finished in "suede" lacquer. The legs are in bronze. It was produced as a limited edition of 30 pieces signed by Andrée Putman. Height: (open) 114cm (closed) 81cm Width: 120 cm Depth: 38cm • The "T" stool, top right, created by Pierre Chareau (c.1927). The seat can be solid black-stained mahogany or rosewood veneer; the structure is patinated steel. Height: 48cm Width: 49cm Depth: 38.5cm • A floor lamp by Mariano Fortuny (1907) in black lacquered steel and chrome-plated brass, right, with a black and white umbrella shade. It takes a 300W bulb. Height: 196cm min. Width: 91cm Depth: 82cm • A folding table by Ecart Design, below right. The top is of high-lustre black-lacquered medium density fibreboard, with a black-stained beech structure. Height: (folded) 80.5cm (open) 57cm Width: (folded) 8cm 41cm

Side table and console from the "Equerre" collection (1995) in varnished African walnut, left. The tops, which pivot, incorporate drawers in patinated varnished metal sheet. The base of the side table is of patinated varnished metal tube and metal sheet. Height: 50cm, 74cm, Width: 51cm, 110.5cm, Depth: 32cm, 51cm • Clothes rack in chromed and lacquered anthracite grey steel tube, created for Les 3 Suisses in 1985, below. Height: 184-210cm, Width: 122cm, Depth: 60cm

This piece of furniture with glass shelves, above, was designed for the CIRVA. The irregularly-shaped display niches use different pieces of glass. It is made up of found objects: electric insulators, iron bars and glass remnants which have been thrown away because they are no longer useful. • Variation of a desk and standard lamp from the "Kraft" collection, designed in 1989 for Les 3 Suisses, right. The lamps are of lacquered steel tubes and plates, with brass escutcheon plates and butterfly screws. The height of the shades is adjustable. Height: 45cm, 117cm, Diameter of shade 45cm, 56cm, Depth: 53cm, 71cm

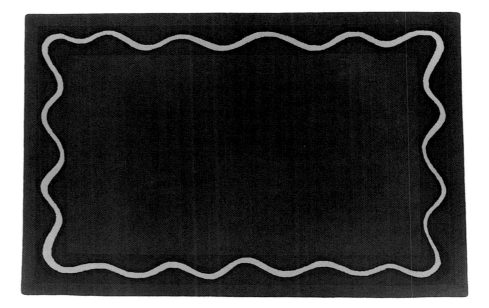

These pure wool rugs were designed by Andrée Putman and are distributed by Toulemonde Bochart. "Come" (1989), above, measures 180 x 270cm and is edited by Ecart International. "Voie Lactée", left, depicts the canopy of heaven with stardust, galaxies, North and South etc. It was created in 1994 as a special edition. "Ecriture" (1995), below, measures 300 x 200cm and is edited by Ecart International.

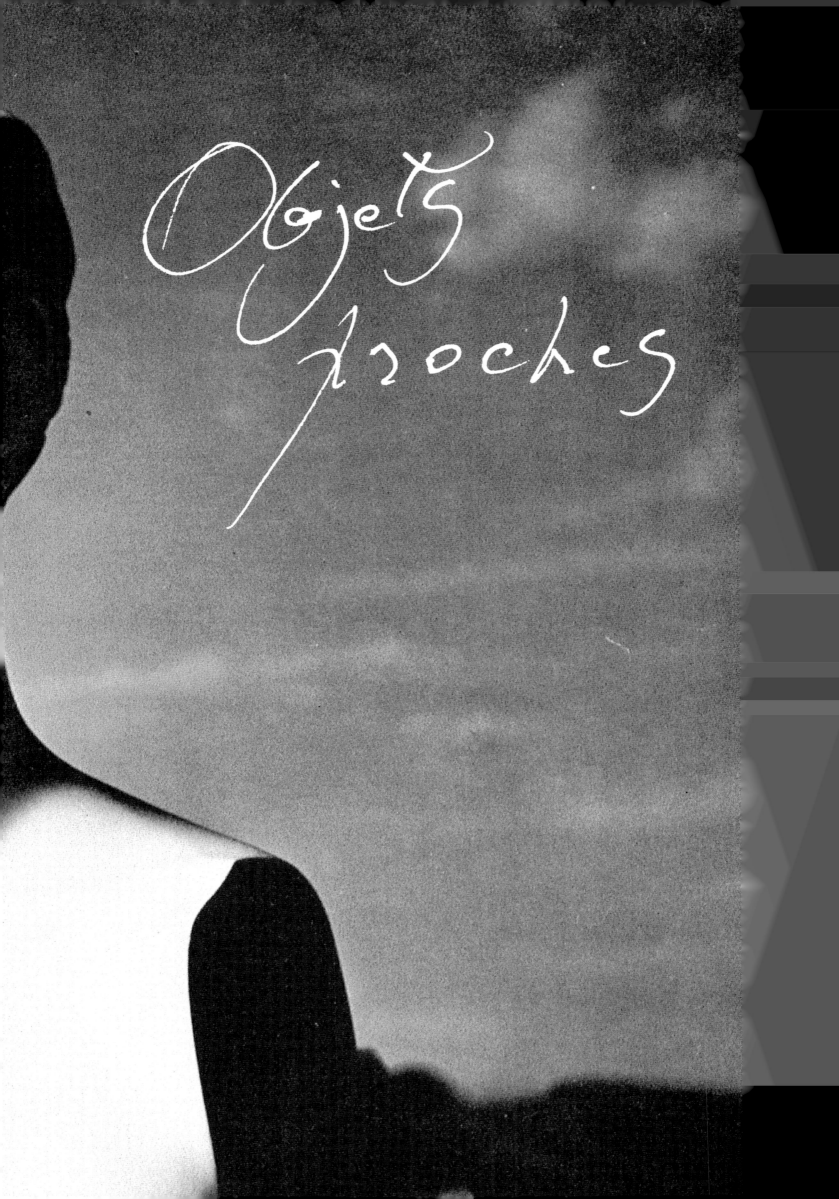

OBJECTS IN CLOSE-UP

Ecart pays close attention to detail because there is no such thing
as a scale of importance: everything is of equal consequence in a
project. The drawing office is therefore often compelled to
improvise using new materials, to design something which
cannot be found in the shops. There can be nothing more
exhilarating than to design everything, down to the texture of a
fabric or the exact shade of a moquette, the colour of a piece of
porcelain or the motif for a carpet, after devising a type of
lighting in relation to the climate or a window in relation to the
brightness of the sun; nothing more exciting than the possibility
in a place like a hotel or an office, as in a house, of concentrating
on the smallest detail. Ecart's abilities and its talent for extending
its philosophy of "the soul of a place" to materials and everyday
objects, have led the company to pursue activities in the field of
styling and product design.

PREVIOUS SPREAD

*Andrée Putman's mannequin for
Pucci.*

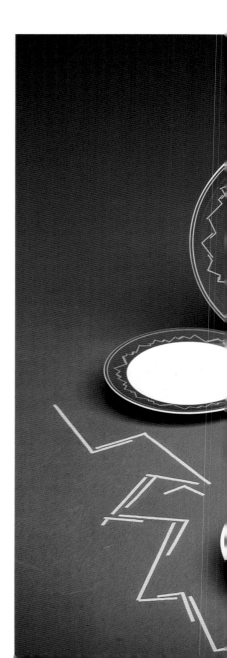

Andrée Putman's two porcelain collections for Ancienne Manufacture Royale: "Barettes Royales" and "Lune", left.
• The "Damier" collection for Ancienne Manufacture Royale, far left. Colour has been introduced at unexpected and irregular intervals into a traditional black and white chequered pattern. Confusion has replaced orderliness to imbue this collection with rhythm and verve.
• Below and below right, tableware designed in 1987 and distributed in the United States by Sasaki, including a complete table service, glasses and a tea service.
• Right, coral version of the "Tressage" collection for Ancienne Manufacture Royale. Trompe l'oeil effects have introduced a touch of humour into the collection. The coral finish creates the illusion of weaving, whether gauze, knitting or meshwork.

Far left, floor lamp from the "Pampille" collection for Baccarat. The stem is of sycamore on a matt nickel-plated metal, glass and sycamore base. The shade is opal glass on a matt nickel-plated frame, with clear-cut crystal pendants. • Adjustable suspension light from the "Pampille" collection, left. Opal glass shade with matt nickel-plated frame, fibre cord and matt nickel-plated metal canopy and pulley system. The counter-weights are clear crystal balls covered with steel beads. • Pocket ashtray in titanium, below left, from the "Blend" collection designed for Swedish Company.

Below left, small clock designed for Paris-Musée. The metal sphere has a catch in the shape of a small leaf. When open, it reveals a face whose wreath of leaves is surrounded by the numbers of the watch. There are three versions: gold, silver and black.

Above, "Monnaie de Paris", a rocaille-style set of jewellery including ring, brooch, bracelet, earrings and necklace. Its multi-faceted appearance is created by the differing treatment of the precious metal surface which does not react uniformly to the light.

Above, small lacquered metal folding table with removable tray, created for Les 3 Suisses.
• The "Wing Shoe", right, a collector's miniature shoe designed for Charles Jourdan.
•"La Nuit" Krug champagne bucket and flutes, below. "When my friends the Krugs asked me to dream up 'une mise en lumière' for their celebrated champagne, I wanted to create a design shimmering with surprises, where light bounced magically, as if from a mirrored ball."

Table created for Les 3 Suisses. Round tables do not usually fit into corners. This one, with castors and two folding leaves, has been designed to fit easily into the corner of a room.

Rug, "Moderato Cantabile", from the "Adagio" collection for Toulemonde Bochart. The design makes explicit reference to Andrée Putman's early music studies at the Paris Conservatoire.

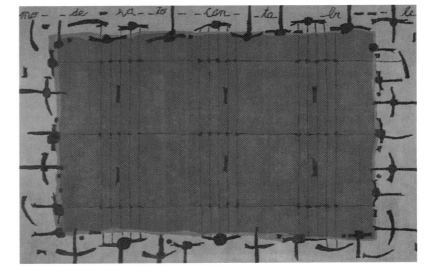

187

Bench from the "Entrepôts Lainé" collection, designed by Andrée Putman for Tectona, a French garden furniture manufacturer, and comprising benches and a table. It is made of teak laths, with aluminium legs. Length: 150, 190 and 240cm.

A lamp designed for the Gitane Foundation in 1992. The structure is metallic and the shade is of parchment.

Collaborators

The following were Andrée Putman's collaborators on projects for Ecart:

1978
Thierry Mugler shop, Paris: Jean-François Bodin, Juan Lazzaro

1980 - 1984
Yves St Laurent shops, USA: Jean-François Bodin, Bruno Moinard

1981
Stan Levy and Colette Bel apartment, Paris: Jean-François Bodin, Bruno Moinard
Hémisphères shop, Paris: Jean-François Bodin, Bruno Moinard

1982
Taubman apartment, Detroit: Jean-François Bodin, Bruno Moinard
Karl Lagerfeld office, Paris: Jean-François Bodin, Bruno Moinard
Apartment, Paris: Jean-François Bodin, Bruno Moinard
Karl Lagerfeld apartment, Rome: Jean-François Bodin, Bruno Moinard

1983
Michel Guy apartment, Paris: Jean-François Bodin, Bruno Moinard
Morgans Hotel, New York, room mock-up for the Salon des Artistes Décorateurs, Paris: Jean-François Bodin, Bruno Moinard

1984
Centre d'Arts Plastiques Contemporain (CAPC) Bordeaux: Jean-François Bodin, Bruno Moinard, Antoine Dumont
Parts of Barney's department store, New York: Jean-François Bodin, Bruno Moinard, André Burgos
Morgans Hotel, New York: Jean-François Bodin, Bruno Moinard
Karl Lagerfeld shop, Paris: Jean François Bodin, Bruno Moinard
Azzedine Alaïa salon, Melbourne: Jean-François Bodin, Bruno Moinard

1985
Ecart International showroom and offices, Paris: Jean-François Bodin, Bruno Moinard
Ecart offices, Paris: Jean-François Bodin, Bruno Moinard
M. Jack Lang, Minister of Culture, office, Paris: Bruno Moinard, Thierry Conquet
Editions du Regard offices, Paris: Jean-François Bodin, Bruno Moinard
United Nations Plaza and Metropolitan Tower model apartments, New York: Bruno Moinard, Thierry Conquet

Azzedine Alaïa salon and showroom, Paris: Jean-François Bodin, Bruno Moinard
M. Galinier-Warrain, Director of Lancôme, office, Paris: Bruno Moinard
Karl Lagerfeld showroom, New York: Jean-François Bodin, Bruno Moinard
Karl Lagerfeld shops, London, Melbourne and Toronto: Jean-François Bodin, Bruno Moinard

1986
St James Club, Paris: Bruno Moinard, Antoine Dumont
Ebel stand for Trade Fair, Basel: Bruno Moinard, Thierry Conquet
Didier Grumbach apartment, Paris: Bruno Moinard, Flavie Austruit
Rosenberg apartment, New York: Bruno Moinard, Thierry Conquet

1987
Joe Pytka's studio, Los Angeles: Thierry Conquet, André Burgos
Ferrari show for Cartier Foundation, Jouy-en-Josas: Bruno Moinard
Ecart bathroom, Paris: Bruno Moinard, Flavie Austruit
Ebel shop, London: Thierry Conquet, Laurent Buttazzoni
Ebel offices in Le Corbusier's Villa Turque, La Chaux-de-Fonds: Thierry Conquet, Laurent Buttazzoni
M. Chaban-Delmas and ministers, offices at the Hôtel de Région, Bordeaux: Bruno Moinard, Thierry Conquet

1988
Metropolitan Home interior contributed in aid of AIDS research, New York: Bruno Moinard, André Burgos
Ebel shop, place Vendôme, Paris: Thierry Conquet, Laurent Buttazzoni
Ebel head office, New York: Thierry Conquet, André Burgos
Ebel shop, Milan: Thierry Conquet, Laurent Buttazzoni
Carita Institute, Paris: Bruno Moinard, Dominique Boissinot-Verger, Elliott Le Roi Barnes, Frédéric Lavaud, Caroline Schmidt
Christophe von Weyhe apartment, Paris: Bruno Moinard

1989
Ebel shop, New York: Thierry Conquet, Elliott Le Roi Barnes
Ministry of Finance, two of the four ministerial offices, Paris: Bruno Moinard, Antoine Dumont
Balenciaga salon, Paris: Bruno Moinard, Flavie Austruit

Balenciaga, new design concept for shops worldwide: Bruno Moinard, Flavie Austruit
Rights of Man office, Fifteenth Summit of the Industrialized Nations, floors 34, 35 and main access areas, Grande Arche de la Défense, Paris: Thierry Conquet, Marie-Anne Martinot-Lagarde, Daniela Pugger
Au Bon Marché department store, Paris: Bruno Moinard
Le Lac Hotel, near Tokyo: Bruno Moinard, Flavie Austruit
Ebel shop, Zurich: Thierry Conquet, Laurent Buttazzoni
Wasserturm Hotel, Cologne: Bruno Moinard, Georges Grenier, Cardine Schmidt

1990
Froment Putman Gallery, Paris: Bruno Moinard, Frédéric Lavaud
Bureau de Direction, Belgium: Bruno Moinard, Frédéric Lavaud
Ebel Suisse showroom, Hardhof: Thierry Conquet, Laurent Buttazzoni

1991
"Les Années VIA" exhibition, Musée des Arts Décoratifs, Paris: Bruno Moinard, Frédéric Lavaud
Ecart offices, Paris: Bruno Moinard
Georges Rech shop, London: Bruno Moinard, Flavie Austruit, Yann Piller
Man Woman shop, Manchester: Bruno Moinard, Patsy Enelow
Isy Brachot Gallery, Paris: Bruno Moinard, Frédéric Lavaud
La Sept (Channel 7) offices, Paris: Bruno Moinard, Flavie Austruit, Marie-Anne Martinot-Lagarde, Sophie Rasse

1992
"In Black and White" exhibition, Wexner Center for the Arts, Columbus, Ohio: Bruno Moinard, Elliott Le Roi Barnes
James Brown apartment, Paris: Laurent Buttazzoni, Bruno Moinard
Cacharel Enfants shop, Barcelona: Bruno Moinard, Laurent Buttazzoni
Musée des Beaux Arts, Rouen: Bruno Moinard, Antoine Dumont, Sophie Rasse
Orchid Club House, Kobé: Bruno Moinard, Frédéric Lavaud
Salon d'Honneur and restaurant, French pavilion, World Exposition, Seville: Bruno Moinard, Elliott Le Roi Barnes, Delphine Braud
Jean-Paul Goude's house, Paris: Marie-Anne Martinot Lagarde, Flavie Austruit, Laurent Buttazzoni, Bruno Moinard

Private Villa, Belgium: Bruno Moinard, Laurent Buttazzoni

1993
Air France Concorde: Flavie Austruit, Bruno Moinard, Nazak Maniei
Bally, Zurich, Cologne and Geneva: Gilles Leborgne, Veronika Pabst, Nathalie du Luart, Laurent Buttazzoni
Karl Lagerfeld's studio, Paris: Laurent Buttazzoni

1993-1994
Offices, Avenue Montaigne, Paris: Sophie Rasse, Flavie Austruit, Bruno Moinard

1994
Total, La Défense, Paris: Marion Guidoni, Gilles Leborgne
Hôtel du Département, Des-Bouches-du-Rhône, Marseilles: Gilles Leborgne, Elliott Le Roi Barnes, Marion Guidoni, Veronika Pabst
"Le Bureau" restaurant, Gildo Pastor Centre, Monaco: Elliott Le Roi Barnes, Olivier Lempereur
Et Vous, Paris: Bruno Moinard, Olivier Lempereur
Lee apartment and gallery, Paris: Elliott Le Roi Barnes
Andrée Putman's apartment, Paris: Frédéric Lavaud

1995
Sheraton Hotel, Roissy: Delphine Vendel, Bruno Moinard, Nathalie du Luart
Connolly, London: Bruno Moinard, Elliott Le Roi Barnes
Peter Greenaway's "The Pillow Book": Marion Guidoni, Frédéric Lavaud

1996
Morgan's Hotel, New York (refurbishment): Laurent Buttazzoni

Credits

Andrée Putman, Ecart, the author and the publishers would like to thank the following for the use of their photographs:

Peter Allen 186 centre (pocket ashtray)
Josef Astor 182-3
Alexandre Bailhache 159
Gabriele Basilico 132 left
Patricia Canino 6, 19, 67 top and bottom, 70, 71, 80
    and 81 top, 82 left and right, 83 left and right, 84, 85,
    112-13, 114-15, 115 bottom, 120 left, 120-1, 121
    right, 122, 123 left and right, 134-5, 136, 137 left and
    right, 140, 141 top, centre and bottom, 151, 164,
    164-5, 165 right, 180 bottom right, 187 top left and
    right
Dominique Cohas 184 top left, 185 top
J.M. Dauba 138, 139 top and bottom, 150
Jacques Dirand 73, 146 top and bottom, 150, 162, 163
Todd Eberle 26, 27,
K. Fitzsimons 50-1, 52-3
Richard Foster 130 top and bottom
Don Freeman 186 bottom left
Rainer Gaertner 32-33, 34 bottom
Nicholas Gentilli & Associates 126, 127
Jean-Pierre Godeau 155 top and bottom
Vincent Godeau 10-11
Marc Guillaumot 168-9, 171 top, centre and bottom
Lyu Hanabusa 38-9, 41
Charles Jourdan 187 centre
Christoph Kicherer 62-3, 63 bottom, 98 left and right,
    189
Karl Lagerfeld 156
Peter Mauss 119
Nacasa & Partners 42, 43, 102-3, 104-5 top, 105
    bottom
Paul Raftery 89, 90, 91 left
Dominique Sarraute 186 bottom right
J.M. Tardy 55 top
Robert Terzian 180 top left
Deidi von Schaewen 14-15, 22-3, 24 top and bottom,
    28 left and right, 29, 30 top, 30-1, 34 top, 35, 36, 37,
    40 top, 44, 45 top, left and right, 47, 48 left and
    right, 49 top and bottom, 54, 55 bottom, 56-7, 58
    top and bottom, 59 top and bottom, 60, 61 top and
    bottom, 66-7, 68-9, 72 right and left, 74, 75, 76, 77,
    78 top, centre and bottom, 79, 86, 87 top, 92, 92-3,
    93 top, 94-5, 96-7, 106-7, 107 bottom, 108-9, 111
    top and bottom, 116, 117, 118, 131 top, centre and
    bottom, 132 right, 133 top and bottom (?), 142-3,
    144-5, 145 right, 147 left and right, 148, 149 left and
    right, 152, 152-3, 157 right and bottom, 160, 161
    top and bottom, 166, 167 top and bottom, 176 top
    left and right, 177 top and third from top, 180 top
    right and bottom left, 181 top, centre and bottom,
    186 top left and right, 187 bottom left and right
Simon/Agence Vu 110
Paul Warchol 20-21, 25
Jonty Wilde 124-5

All line and wash drawings, all photographs in the
Editions chapter and the following, © reserved: 64-5, 99
top and bottom, 128, 129, 154, 158 top and bottom.

Index

Selling to
Affluent
WOMEN

Selling to
Affluent
WOMEN

Face-to-face
with Today's
Big Spenders

Marti Barletta

Paramount Market Publishing, Inc.

Paramount Market Publishing, Inc.
274 North Goodman Street STE D-214
Rochester, NY 14607

Phone: 607-275-8100

www.paramountbooks.com

Publisher: James Madden
Editorial Director: Doris Walsh
Copyright © 2014 Marti Barletta

This publication is designed to provide accurate and authoritative information in regard to the subject matter covered. It is sold with the understanding that the publisher is not engaged in rendering legal, accounting, or other professional services. If legal advice or other expert assistance is required, the services of a competent professional should be sought.

All trademarks are the property of their respective companies.

ISBN-13: 978-1-941688-28-1 | ISBN-10: 1-941688-28-4

Contents

Introduction

Today's most successful sales professionals are not only well-versed in the specifics of their sophisticated products; they are also adept at reading people. In response to the greater diversity of populations everywhere, I'll bet that somewhere along the line you've received training to help you recognize and adapt to the norms, attitudes and behaviors of prospects from other cultures.

Would it surprise you to learn that in many ways, "female gender culture" is as different from what men think of as "the norm" as India is from Italy? Sure, people are people, and from one perspective, Indians have more in common with Italians than they have differences. No matter what culture we're from, we all eat, speak, sleep, smile, bathe, bake and enjoy music, to mention a few. But *what* we eat, *how* we speak, *where* we sleep – all of these are done differently in different cultures.

Likewise, men and women – of the same culture and in general around the world – have more commonalities than differences. But the tricky thing is that for the most part, we don't recognize gender differences as being relevant to how we interact with each other.

But they are actually more than just "relevant." They are the key to whether we feel liked, respected, listened to, understood and appreciated by the person we're interacting with. And as you look over that list – aren't those the exact qualities needed to create the rapport with prospects and clients that will earn you their trust?

Here's the deal: Until you understand and adapt to the expectations and priorities of your female prospects, you are unlikely to be as successful doing business with them as you are with male prospects.

And here's the problem with that: **Women have most of the money.**

A few "financial factoids" for your consideration:

- ⊃ Women represent **43 percent of the wealthiest individuals** in the U.S. ($1.5 million or more). (*IRS statistics cited by the New York Times*)

- ⊃ In 2000, the Federal Reserve reported that women controlled 51.3 percent **of U.S. wealth.** (*PBS*). Now, **they control nearly 60 percent**. (Virginia Tech, *Women in Leadership & Philanthropy*)

- ⊃ In 2005, women donated **$21.7 billion to charity, 29 percent more** than the $16.8 billion donated by men. (*IRS data analyzed by accounting firm Grant Thornton*)

- ⊃ **Two-thirds of JPMorgan's philanthropic services clients** are women. (*US News & World Report*)

So I think it's fair to say that women warrant your attention.

"That's fine," you may say. "I get it. Women want to be treated the same way a man is treated."

Actually, no.

That's the irony and the disconnect. Women themselves often don't realize how signals from one gender culture get garbled in transmission to someone of the other gender. Unless the sender and the receiver are on the same frequency, there's likely to be a certain amount of static interference, which in turn can lead to some unfortunate misunderstandings.

The reality is, **if you treat a new female client exactly the same way as you treat your best male clients, chances are she will walk out of your meeting feeling patronized, her priorities ignored and her questions unanswered.**

And nobody's got time for that, right?

Here's the good news: **Going after this "market with the money" is not that hard.** Truly. A handful of new insights and maybe ten basic behavior changes should set you well on your way.

By the time you finish this book, you'll know how to:

- Identify top women prospects and bring yourself to their attention.
- Introduce yourself and follow through with relationship-building activities.
- Discover what she's looking for in a product and persuade her to consider yours.
- Overcome "decision reluctance" and close the sale.
- Keep your investment in this customer paying off for you over and over again.

1
Prospecting

The amount of prospecting that sales professionals have to do varies considerably from industry to industry. People who sell computers, consumer electronics, or telecommunications products really don't need this skill; their customers come to them. Customers come to car dealers, too, but the more sophisticated salespeople take the initiative to actively cultivate prospects on their own.

However, **the real pros at prospecting are the people in the financial services industries — banking, investments, and insurance.** Building up their book of business requires making a very wide range of contacts and having the skill to convert a high percentage of prospects into customers. Let's start with ideas for making contacts among women prospects.

Do You Know Your Prime Prospects?

When you're in the money business, your best prospects are people who have a lot of it. OK, so that's no surprise. And as we just saw, women actually control the majority of the financial assets in this country. But which women? Who and where are they? And how do you meet them?

They're not who you think they are. Most beginners in the high-net-worth women's market assume "wealthy women" is synonymous with "wealthy widows," and so that's the first market – and sometimes even the only market – they look to. Certainly, there are wealthy widows looking for financial advice (see below) but they're not the only females with funds. As you'll see, there are actually a number of sub-markets of affluent women.

Working Women

We'll start with working women because a study done by The Economist Intelligence Unit for Barclay's Wealth in the U.K. found that, rather than acquiring their riches through marriage, inheritance or wealth, **80 percent of women had earned their riches themselves.** (*The Economist*)

The executive suite. One place people look when they're trying to identify affluent women prospects is in the executive suite, probably because of all the press coverage top corporate women get. (Although their ranks are growing fast, women like Melissa Mayer, Indra Nooyi and Ursula Burns are still kind of a novelty.) This is a good place to look – in fact, over 50 percent of managers in U.S. business are women – but it's not the end of the road. While there are certainly lots of women earning big corporate paychecks, there are two other categories that I would look at as well: women in professional practice and women business owners.

Professional practice. If you work in the high-net-worth market, chances are you already know which are the high-paying professions. But it may surprise you to learn how many of these professions have women-specific associations. In the medical field, for instance, there are American associations of women dentists, emergency physicians, psychiatrists, radiologists, and surgeons. These organizations generally exist to address non-medical issues (they have access to medical information through the "general" association) and may welcome an offer to provide their members with some worthwhile insight on managing their money, whether at the local chapter or the national conference.

Women business owners (WBOs). The fastest-growing segment of women-owned businesses is the sector with 100 or more employees – and presumably the greatest investment needs. Not surprisingly, the $1 million women-owned businesses differ from smaller women-owned businesses in a number of ways, including: They are more likely to use formal advisors such as accountants (40.7 percent vs. 28.9 percent), lawyers (15.7 percent vs. 6.6 percent), and boards of directors (13.3 percent vs. 4.6 percent), and less likely to use informal financial advisors such as family or friends (21.7 percent vs. 35.5 percent).

A full 72 percent of women business owners have investments in stocks, bonds, or mutual funds compared to 58 percent of women employees. These aren't the local Tupperware ladies chatting it up on Wednesday nights. You'll find them where you find the other well-to-do business owners – chambers of commerce and philanthropic boards, for example.

Another advantage of seeking out women business owners is the opportunity to cross- and up-sell to them. The vast majority (86 percent) of women business owners say that they use some of the same brands of products and services – such as telecommunications services and insurance – in both their business and their household, and that this is a conscious decision based on quality, convenience, discounts, and experience with the company.

Wealthy Widows

You know, no doubt, that right now, the largest intergenerational transfer of wealth in history is taking place as the Baby Boomers inherit from their high-saving parents. He inherits from his parents, she inherits from hers. And then, life expectancies being what they are, she inherits his assets too.

The average age of widowhood in the U.S. is 67 years old. And thanks to that difference in life expectancy and the common convention of women marrying men older than they are, women tend to outlive their husbands by 15-18 years. This means that for almost two decades, the combined wealth of two generations and three families is in her hands.

Most of today's older women grew up before the recent dramatic advances in women's social and economic roles. For most of them, women didn't work outside the home, and they generally didn't get involved with big-ticket decisions. (Remember the good old days when a husband treated his wife to a washing machine on their fifth anniversary?) Financial advisors built strong relationships with the man of the house but rarely involved his wife.

So who manages the family assets after the husband passes on? An executive from a large financial firm mentioned recently at a conference that **close to 70 percent of widows change financial advisors within three years of their husband's death.** With no existing bond with the family advisor to hold them back, the widows walked. The moral of the story is this: When you're working with "married" money, make sure you build relationships with *both* the husband and wife.

The point here is that there are lots of prospects out there, and **you know what the kicker is? Affluent women are almost never prospected!**

The Kicker

When I started working with financial services companies, I'd been in my career for 19 years, I was a vice president at a large marketing agency, had a nice salary, and had almost never been contacted by a financial services advisor. (If I'd been prospected twice, that was a big year.)

When I realized this, I asked numerous female colleagues of similar rank and salary what their experience had been – and it was always similar to my own. Meanwhile, our male colleagues of similar rank and salary got contacted frequently. At least half of the senior executives at my company were women. Thus, at least half of the prospecting pool was being overlooked. How could that be?

Here's the kicker to the kicker: One financial services guy did contact me that year, and he now has all of our family's accounts. And he was smart and nice and both my husband and I liked him. Was our decision to move our combined assets to this advisor a shared/joint decision? Of course. But I was the one who was eager to take action, and it was my initiative to take the meeting and see what he had to offer. In other words, he called me and got an audience, while everyone else was calling my husband, and getting ignored.

An even more dramatic example: One of my financial service clients asked me to do a survey among high net worth women – those with investable assets over $1 million. I spoke with a woman who was one of the eight top executives of a start-up company that had recently been acquired. Each of these eight executives came away from the acquisition with several million dollars for their shares. Shortly thereafter, all seven of her male colleagues were deluged with prospecting contacts from people who wanted to help them manage the huge chunk of money they'd received. She was "deluged" with exactly two.

Wow! Obviously **lots** of people (enough for a "deluge!") saw this list and decided that seven of the executives were worth contacting – while the other one, a woman, wasn't. What were they thinking?

And – Are you thinking what I'm thinking? This market is wide open and waiting for someone to seize the opportunity!

Place Yourself Where She Can See You

Another way to prospect is to boost your visibility and credibility in such a way that your prospects, suitably impressed, come to you.

Free media (PR). One way to make yourself visible and garner favorable attention is by contributing articles and relevant information to the websites and publications your prospects read. Two things make this a great marketing idea. First, you'll get the visibility you want. If you target "affluent women who need a will" as your market, for instance, you might write a regular column called Family Matters that discusses the financial and tax implications of estate planning *in the context of the personal considerations* she is likely to be trying to address.

Submit your article to a targeted magazine like *Today's Chicago Woman* or *Sheridan Road* (for you Second City citizens) or a newsletter for a women's professional association. Second, there's minimal competition; most of these types of publications are *looking* for content that is relevant and useful to their readers.

Paid media (advertising). Mind your message, and your media placement. A "concierge accountant" trying to reach women in prosperous communities placed ads in the business section of several of the local community newspapers serving the wealthiest suburbs in his metro area. Nothing. No response.

He asked several of his female neighbors what was going on. Was the message wrong? Was the "concierge accountant" concept unappealing for some reason? "Oh, no," they told him, "We get our business news from the major media outlets. When we read the community paper, we mostly look just in the school or lifestyle sections."

He moved his media accordingly, and the phone started ringing. Counter-intuitive? Not at all – when you understand that busy women with work and household responsibilities prioritize their reading by "What do I need to know *right now*?"

2

Networking:
Choose and Schmooze

Personal connection. Women are more likely than men to volunteer, so one way to create personal visibility is by volunteering in community services organizations, serving on boards of directors, and otherwise participating in the community, as we briefly discussed above.

Community outreach. Offer information to groups of women: approach existing organizations or groups and offer to speak on your area of expertise. There's an assumption that you must be good if the executive director or president is inviting you; otherwise surely she wouldn't do so! These are women who already have something in common, if only the group, and also probably know each other fairly well and trust each other already. Therefore, word of mouth spreads particularly quickly and well.

Once you've found the organizations that have high concentrations of the people you're trying to reach, the next step is to network with those organizations and the people within them. Even "general interest" organizations like Rotary, the Optimist Club, professional associations, community groups, local and regional leadership organizations, and so on, while predominantly male, have substantial percentages of female members.

The day-to-day reality of making contacts and building rela-tionships is that people naturally tend to network with others like themselves. Men network with men, women with women – some-times it's just easier to talk to someone else who has the same lan-guage and customs as you do. But the upshot is something that has important implications for male networkers.

Women in a world of men are invisible. One of my woman friends, a regional director at a major insurance company, was training a salesman to be an insurance agent. He wasn't fresh out of school; in fact, this man was mature, confident, and fairly sea-soned as a worker. During his training he accompanied her to a networking event – a meeting of the local chamber of commerce. At this meeting, she observed that although 25 to 30 percent of the attendees were women, he didn't talk to any of them.

After the meeting, she said to him, "I was interested to note that you're meeting and greeting – just not with any of the women." His response? "Oh, were there women there?" She laughed and said, "Sure there were. There were 15 or 20 of them." Apparently, something in his internal software was registering the women in the room as "background noise." Whatever the reason, the point is that even face-to-face with the physical reality, 25 to 30 percent of this networking opportunity was invisible to him.

Men in a world of women are apprehensive. In New York, there is a well-established organization called the Financial Wom-en's Association (FWA). It has about 850 members, mostly high-level women involved in the financial services industry. I was told that about 10 percent of the members of the FWA are men.

At one of its breakfast meetings, with 150 people in attendance, I sat at a table with one man and seven women. I heard someone ask the guy if he felt odd surrounded by a majority of women. He acknowledged that at first he had been concerned that he might feel left out, but he'd been attending now for several years and had always found the women to be welcoming and engaging. As a matter of fact, when the woman who was chairing the breakfast meeting welcomed the attendees, she made a special point of welcoming the men.

The truth is that when you're trying to network with women, apprehensions are understandable – but unnecessary. Because female gender culture is inclusive and egalitarian, women are inclusive and welcoming to men in their midst. Their view of men coming into these professional organizations tends to be very positive.

Rather than slanting toward wondering what he is doing invading their territory, most women feel: *Finally! Here's a man who is taking us seriously and treating us like any other professional association.* By attending, you're signaling respect. If you make the choice to participate, you won't stick out like a sore thumb; you'll stand out in positive ways – because many of your male colleagues are not doing this. You are a pioneer, a maverick, way out in the forefront.

Join the Party. At any networking event, a lot of us find it hard to approach a group of people we don't know and introduce ourselves. When a man approaches a group of women, he might feel the added apprehension of whether he'll know what to talk about. What if the women are talking about shoes and jewelry? What if they're talking about labor and delivery?

And they may well be. Appalling as it may seem to men, women among women can shift from business to personal – from prepping for a big meeting to panty hose that run when you have no time to deal with it – and the conversation can get really personal, really fast. So men worry that if the women are in the middle of some intensively engaging topic, they may not drop it when the men approach. Then what will the men say? They can hardly share their own panty hose war stories, now can they?

In fact, it may be true that women won't always instantly change the subject, but they will rapidly acknowledge men and actively find ways to bring them into the discussion. Women are "groups" people and "people" people. If the guy wants to be a part of the group, he will be welcomed in.

Seminar Selling

Like networking, seminar selling is an often-used tactic when you're building up business. The typical way of doing seminar selling is to get as many people into the room as possible, with the expectation that of any given 50 people in a room, 1 or 2 will become live prospects. It's because of this low conversion ratio, of course, that you try to get the maximum number of people into the room.

With women, though, there's a more productive way to go about this: Have smaller seminars and higher conversion ratios. Instead of getting 50 into a classroom, go for 10 around a conference table – if the 10 are women.

Linda Denny, who rose through the ranks from insurance agent to regional director to corporate vice president at New York Life, came up with this innovation when she was helping regional offices all over the country recruit more women into an insurance career at her company. Ten or so women who had been referred to the local office as interested in learning more about insurance sales were invited to participate with a group of other women in an exploratory discussion about the career. So the size of the group was considerably smaller than is typical.

The second departure from standard practice was this: Instead of Linda talking while the "audience" passively listened, she would start with each person introducing herself and saying a little about why she was there. When Linda talked about her personal background, she made a point of sharing anecdotes illustrating why she had found being an agent such a satisfying career.

As each woman introduced herself, she would do the same: Linda asked them to say a few words about who they were, what they did, what they loved about their current job, and what they'd change if they could. She calls this "kitchen table recruiting," because the feeling is a little like a group of girlfriends sitting around the kitchen table with a cup of coffee for a couple of hours.

Very quickly the women in the room get to know each other, and the conversation becomes candid. Linda would keep her ears open for opportunities to comment on how a career with her company provided something the prospect was looking for or resolved a problem at her current position.

For instance, a participant might say that she loved being an emergency room nurse because she could help people when they needed it the most. In response, Linda might say, "That's one of the things I love about my job, too; when someone's just had a tragedy, I can come to her door and deliver a policy benefit check so that she doesn't have to add financial worries to everything else she's dealing with at a time like that."

Linda's experience has been that it's not at all unusual to get three to five interested and well-qualified prospects out of only ten participants with this approach.

The reason is that she has made it a personalized experience, selling the career by making it relevant to each individual woman in the room. Instead of **talking *at*** her, she has **listened *to*** her and her comments have helped the prospect understand how the career connects with her life.

It's not hard to translate this approach from recruiting to sales. Instead of sending out direct mail invitations to every woman in the neighborhood inviting her to a seminar on hedge funds – and hoping that the room is packed – use networking skills and your contacts to invite ten women to a "private investment workshop." Tell each to bring a list of two or three questions, as the workshop will be small and interactive, and you'd be happy to answer individual questions. As you answer, of course, you're learning more and more about what is important to the prospect and, at the same time, demonstrating what a whiz you are and what you would be like to work with.

Some consultants set this up as a three-part series, held on-site for a group of participants who work at the same company. The series approach gives you and the participants several chances to get to know each other and further boosts the likelihood of turning a prospect into a customer.

Do Women Prefer to Work with Female Advisors?

At my sales training seminars, I'm often asked whether women customers prefer to work with female financial consultants. The answer is "not really."

It's true that professional women often like to support other professional women by trying to include them in any search for a new advisor – doctor, lawyer, accountant, and so on. But once she starts interviewing them to decide with whom she wants to work, it's a completely level playing field. Competence and chemistry count a lot more than gender. Your competence in the field is up to you, of course, but I can help you with the chemistry. Read on.

Cultivate the Relationship

Let's say you've identified a number of top prospects who happen to be female. Once you've gotten the business card, how do you stay in touch? Lots of business relationships require a period of time to bring to fruition, particularly those where personal trust is one of the keystones of the relationship. For the really high-dollar accounts, getting to know each other is an important part of getting in the game.

Business entertainment. The methods men use to create one-on-one relationships, which work well with other men, simply aren't as comfortable with women. Relationship building often has a social component, and guys build bonds by doing things together, so they might play golf, catch a ball game, or go to a boat show together.

When it's a man and a woman together, the problem is that it looks like a date, it feels like a date, and so even though both people know that it's not a date, they feel awkward. They're just not sure how to behave. The situation is rife with opportunities for miscommunication. Even the little behavioral things get weird: Does he hold the door? Help her with her coat? What is appropriate and what isn't in the business relationship?

Socializing with prospects. An alternative, of course, is to make it a foursome: include the spouses. (This assumes you each have a spouse. If one of you doesn't, then the one-on-one scenario described above gets even weirder.) The good news is that now you're getting to know the husband as well – and it's always good to get to know both. The bad news is that your wife will only want to go out on so many business dates – chances are she has her own commitments, and there are only so many days in the week. Plus, out of courtesy to the two spouses, the outing becomes almost entirely social. Without much chance to even broach the business topic, you've lost half the benefit of business entertainment.

This is all on top of a few simple realities. Although many women play golf, it's not nearly as universal as it is among men. Not as many women are interested in spending an afternoon at a ball game. Men may not be interested, either, but it's part of the expected male culture: men are supposed to be sports fans, and so they go along with it. Women may well go along with it, too – but it won't benefit the relationship if she's regretting the loss of the four hours.

So what do you do, because obviously you still want to get to know women prospects? Here are several suggestions – not the "right" way, just recommendations for alternative ways to get to know women prospects.

Meet women in groups versus one-on-one. Join and participate in organizations where you can interact with women, such as community and volunteer organizations, which are often made up predominantly of women – the PTA, for example. In my hometown, the PTA has 80 committees, 79 of which are chaired by women and 1 by a man: my husband. In situations like this, women feel a sense of comfort and familiarity as you're getting acquainted, and since the focus is on the work you're doing together, the social relationship can develop very naturally without a lot of effort or awkwardness on either side. Soon, word of your particular skill set gets around, people start coming to you for informal advice, and suddenly you've got a prospect.

As it happens, my husband's job doesn't involve prospecting; he volunteered out of a sense of community service. The point is, if he had been prospecting, he would have been in the catbird seat. Does it involve a significant time commitment? Sure it does. But like everything else, what you get out of it depends on what you put into it. Your return is a network of female friends and neighbors who know who you are, what you do, and how well you do it. And you get a network of women who will be quick to refer business to you at every opportunity.

Make your own groups. Create networking events. Women love to network with each other, and they'll love you for picking up the tab. Why not set up a luncheon to talk about a subject pertinent to women? Invite a group of women to attend a museum event with cocktails and conversation afterward. If it includes a fun event, food, and interesting women to chat with, women will attend.

Let's say it's a traveling Impressionist art exhibit – the tickets are limited and hard to get, so you buy 10 or 15 tickets and send out an invitation to a few of your clients inviting them each to bring a friend. The invitations note that cocktails will be served first at the place across from the museum, then the exhibit, then time to chat. Each woman will be delighted to offer her friend this treat; and each woman will be providing a "warm" introduction to another great prospect.

3

The Sales Consultation: Presenting Your Case

All right, we're done with prospecting now, and those of you who went on break because your sales job doesn't involve prospecting can come back into the room and sit down. It's time to consider the sales presentation.

What every customer looks for in a professional advisor is a combination of knowledgeability and trust. We're talking "big trust," as in "with all my worldly goods," **and** "little trust," as in "do you really know what you're talking about or are you just bluffing?" Men and women develop trust in somewhat different ways. Let's talk about how to build trust with women.

Listen More Than You Talk

The first and most important thing I can tell you is this: Talking to women involves a good deal more listening than most men are used to.

Stop "strutting your stuff." One way men earn each other's trust is to communicate their track record. A guy will talk about how good he is as a way of proving he can do a great job: "Half of my clients are worth over a million dollars," he'll say. Or "I doubled his return in six months." They talk about achievements, drop names, and let you know where they stand in the company hierarchy. I call these "credibility displays," because they remind me a little of a peacock who's very proud of his tail feathers.

Don't get me wrong – this is the right thing to do in male gender culture. If you don't, men assume you don't have anything to brag about. But women don't brag, and they don't like it when other people brag. They'll tolerate it quietly, but they won't be impressed. As a matter of fact, rather than building respect, credibility displays are much more likely to ruin rapport.

Listen to her "life story." Why does she launch into her life story when all she wants to do is buy a car? The average male salesperson has a tough time not getting judgmental on this one. As she's explaining to him how many kids she has, she is also telling him how . . .

> they'll use the car to go to the beach on the weekends and for camping in the fall, so of course that means the dog has to come along. . . you wouldn't believe how dirty a dog can get after an afternoon at the beach . . . but most of the time, she'll just be driving to and from work . . . freeway driving you know, so it has to be really reliable . . . and she occasionally needs to drive clients around to look at the houses she's representing so it has to be a pretty decent-looking vehicle.

Ha! Caught you! You were looking at your watch, weren't you?

A lot of salesmen are puzzled by this "life story" thing. When men want to buy a car, they come in and tell you what they're looking for: a four-door sedan with a V-6 engine and antilock brakes. In the immortal words of Lerner and Loewe, "Why can't a woman be more like a man?" Can't she just stay focused on what we're doing here?

Well, she could, but she's trying to help you, believe it or not. First of all, she **is** telling you what she wants in a car, because she's telling you what she's going to use it for. Women think and communicate in both contextual and people terms. You're supposed to be the expert – now that you know what the qualifications are, which cars should she look at? Second, by giving you all this personal information, she is giving you lots of great stuff to work with to build rapport with her. In her culture, if you're a nice person, you'll make a comment or two on something you have in common – the beach, the dog, driving around with clients, it really doesn't matter what. She's giving you a chance to be friendly, for crying out loud – and you're looking at your watch?

Your Turn to Talk

How to present the product. Many corporate sales training programs still teach salespeople to give a canned pitch. There's a set way to present the product, a specific order to discussing its features. The goal is to get in as many good things as you can say about the product before the customer "sidetracks" you with questions. You're missing the point: what she's just told you is not just small talk. She's given you the selling cues you need to persuade her that your product is what she wants.

Don't use the canned pitch; personalize your pitch based on what she's telling you. Explain how the interior of this SUV is designed to be both stylish and easily cleaned – cleaned of sand, for example. Show her how easy it is for anyone, large or small, to climb into the vehicle (just think about those kids and her women clients). Mention that this model has the best repair record in its class, so she won't ever have to worry about being stranded on a freeway. Not only does this tell her you were listening carefully, but it puts all your persuasive points in a context that is much more likely to motivate her to buy.

Pay attention to nonverbal feedback/language. When talking to each other, women generally face each other directly and watch facial expressions and gestures for the extra meaning behind the words. Guys tend to stand at an oblique angle to each other, with both of them looking out in front of them and checking in with each other over their shoulders once in a while.

When women listen to another person, male or female, they use furthering phrases ("I see . . ."), make acknowledgment noises ("Mmm-hmm"), and do a lot of "face work" – smiles and empathetic expressions – to show they're tracking with the conversation and to encourage the speaker to continue.

Think about how a woman sees the body language and non-verbal conventions of male gender culture: Here she is, trying to be friendly, telling you a little about herself, both to build rapport and to give you what you need to help her.

And what do you do? Listen in as she tells her girlfriends how it looked from her perspective:

"He didn't listen to a word I said! He just stood there while I was talking, no reaction, didn't even look at me; he kept looking out over the parking lot. And when I was done, he turned and asked me what kind of car I wanted to look at, right after I just told him!"

Now, obviously, she doesn't understand male gender culture any better than you understood female culture (before you read this book, I mean!). But after all, she is the customer, and you're the one who's supposed to be figuring out how to connect with her. It's actually not that hard, once you know what's going on.

Reading Her Signals Right Can Make or Break Your Rapport with Her

Body Language. Many male sales professionals find it frustrating and annoying to sell to women. One of the biggest complaints men make is they don't have as much success closing women as they do people of their own gender. It generally goes something like this: "I do everything right. I give her tons of good information. I answer questions and I listen. She gives me all the right buying cues, and then I go in for the close. Then she walks out of my office and I never see her again." It's a surprisingly common refrain.

So we ask how he knew the woman prospect was so in sync with his sales presentation. The number one answer is: "She clearly agreed with everything I was saying. She nodded in agreement throughout the whole pitch. That's when I decided to close." And there it is. This is a classic example of communication style misfire.

Answer every question thoroughly. Because of women's more comprehensive buying process, women have a longer list of criteria than men and are voracious information seekers. So no matter how trivial or irrelevant her question may seem to you, answer it.

I realize from your point of view you think you're helping her by keeping the discussion focused on what matters – you're trying to be efficient and may even be trying to be considerate of her time. But if your response to her question is, "Well, that's really not what's important here," you've lost the sale because you've offended the customer. If she says it's important – and if she's talking about it, that's what she's saying – it's important.

One area I've heard several women comment on is salesmen's unwillingness or inability to answer questions on how the product compares to the competition. When my friend Pam was shopping, she asked one salesman, "Why should I buy this car instead of that competitive make and model?" She took it as a given that anyone doing due diligence on such an expensive purchase would compare several options; and in her mind she was giving the salesman an opportunity to showcase his product's advantages. His answer? "You just can't compare the two." "Why not?" she pressed. Again, he said, "You just can't."

This salesman lost the sale because he didn't know his competition as well as she did – and he tried to make her feel dumb for asking a perfectly reasonable question. Interesting sales strategy. Contrast that with the next dealership she went to where they were prepared to answer the same question with details on their product's advantages compared to the competition: newer engine design, more headroom, slightly better gas mileage, and so on.

Don't put down the competition. There's one important qualification to keep in mind as you're applying the advice above. Because of their egalitarian culture, women see any kind of a put-down as inappropriate – "shady dealings." So while it's good to delineate the differences vs. your competitors, don't disparage. "I've heard a lot of complaints about their new model; it just doesn't sound like it's very well made," would be going too far. The key is to keep it neutral, not negative.

Small Courtesies Make Big Points

Good manners are good business with everyone, of course. But with women, good manners that go beyond the basics signal that you are focused on her, not yourself. Small gestures can go a long way; like an auto salesman offering to get her a chair if it seems as if she's had a long day, or getting her kids a couple of sodas from the vending machine because it's such a hot day. But at a recent sales training seminar I was conducting, I realized I had to be a little more specific on this point.

A very experienced and successful salesman came up to me after the seminar and told me how pleased he was with the seminar and all the new stuff he'd learned. He said it had never really occurred to him to do the small courtesies before, but if "sucking up to the client is what it takes to make the sale, I guess I can do that." I thought he was joking at first, but he wasn't.

Coincidentally, later that week I reread a paragraph in Dr. Deborah Tannen's book *You Just Don't Understand!* in which she recounts an instance of a psychologist asking a husband-wife pair of respondents what they thought "politeness" meant. They both happened to answer at the same time: the woman said "consideration for others," and the man said "subservience." I couldn't believe it, but as I asked around among my male acquaintances, it turned out that quite a few men shared this attitude.

Suddenly, I realized that when I was recommending to men that they offer women customers small courtesies, to many of them I was suggesting something completely antithetical to their culture. So now I hasten to add: If you can't do it with genuine sincerity, don't do it at all. Women will see right through you, and instead of having gained her appreciation, you'll have lost her trust.

A Sensitized Population

Nuances and small improvements are especially appreciated by women because of their "extrasensory sensitivity;" they are able to perceive and recall more subtle levels of sight, sound, touch, etc., which means that they are more aware than men of the details of their environment. Similarly, research shows that relative to men, women possess a sort of "emotional X-ray vision;" they pick up on non-verbal signals more precisely, including tone of voice, facial expressions, and body language.

In addition there's an important attitudinal component that magnifies these: Women are a "sensitized population."

At this point, most women, like many people of color, have had enough experience with being slighted or treated inappropriately in certain business situations that they've come to watch for it. Not that they're any more tolerant of it, but forewarned is forearmed, and they've learned to at least be on guard against it. So nowadays, when women have a negative experience with an individual or a business, instead of chalking it up to a careless individual or overall lousy service, they often assume it's because they are female.

For example, car salesmen have a reputation of being condescending to women. I'm sure most of them are not, but the fact of the matter is, almost every woman I've met when the subject comes up has a story to contribute. Regrettably, most of these misunderstandings could be easily avoided.

In reality, both male and female car buyers are going to encounter rude treatment or poor service from time to time. But when men are treated rudely, they don't walk out of the dealership feeling they were treated that way "because they're men." Instead, they think, "That guy's a jerk." But women often chalk up bad behavior to disrespect for women. And the really bad part is, that's what they tell their friends, neighbors, and coworkers about the dealership.

When you consider the dramatic differences in men's and women's interaction styles and combine that with many men's underlying view that small courtesies are expressions of subservience rather than consideration for others, you can see that the situation is rife with opportunities for misunderstanding.

And even innocuous, unintended oversights can easily be perceived by "sensitized populations" to be just one more example of deliberate discourtesy. For example, I think many salesmen are genuinely puzzled by women who get upset over a "little" thing like handing the keys for her test-drive to her husband.

I'm not trying to create an atmosphere of "walking on eggshells" here. Rather, I'm attempting to lay out in very concrete terms how and why an extra dose of sincere consideration and thoughtfulness goes such a long way with women. A little extra reading on the topic and a little focused training for your sales force – both can go a long way toward making sure you get your share of her business.

4
Closing the Sale

The Perfect Answer — A Longer Road

Oddly enough, one of the areas where men and women differ most is in their decision-making styles. Whereas men are looking to make "a good decision," women are looking for "The Perfect Answer." As a result, from women, you can expect a lot more questions, and a longer decision process.

Annoying? Perhaps. Until you understand that in the long run, it's precisely that "deep dive" approach that will cement her commitment to you. She prefers to invest the time upfront to satisfy herself that she's found the right product and the right advisor, so she doesn't have to do it all over again the next time. That means that, relative to your male clients, she is more predisposed to come back to you for her future needs; and she is less likely to abandon you for a "deal of the week" short-term offer elsewhere.

However, it does mean you need to change your expectations and your approach when working with women. Salespeople are trained to try to close the sale in the initial meeting. That may work with men, because they have a faster decision process, and frankly, "shooting from the hip" – that is, making decisions on the spot – is one way they communicate their autonomy and decisiveness. You could call that the "cowboy factor." But women are marksmen, not cowboys – and if you rush them or push them while they're trying to zero in on what they want, all you're going to do is irritate them.

Women want to consider, compare, and talk it over with friends. It's not enough for the product or service to meet her needs; it must be **the best way** to meet her needs. It can be frustrating in this respect, but I'd advise you to refocus your attention on *what you're going to do to follow up* instead of pushing too hard right away. Otherwise, she will start to distrust your motives (you're supposed to be her agent, not her adversary) and destroy all that great rapport I just helped you build up!

Short-circuit decision reluctance. Focus on the benefits of making the decision now – she won't have to make another trip to the office or dealership, for example; or at least all her money won't just be sitting there in a checking account when it could be earning a return, and so on. Motivate her to decide sooner rather than later.

Maybe means maybe. Here's a simple hint that makes a major difference in how you follow up. When men say, "I'll think about it," it's the polite way to say "I'm not interested." But when women say, "I'll think about it," it really means "I'll think about it." Sharon Hadary, former executive director of the Center for Women's Business Research, told me she once made this point in a presentation, and an experienced, successful salesman slapped his hand to his forehead and said: "Oh my God, I'm just realizing how much business I've left on the table over the years because I didn't know that."

You need to follow up with women. Don't just be prepared for a subsequent conversation; expect and plan one. Call her and say, "I was thinking about your concerns, and here's another reason that you should make this decision." To women, this signals a level of connectivity that fits right in with female gender culture – and she'll be responsive to it, I can assure you.

5

Selling to Couples

For men, independence and autonomy are among their highest values. As a corollary, it should come as no surprise that men resist being influenced or directed – especially by women, especially in public. Whereas in women's world a suggestion is seen as an offer of help, in men's minds doing as anyone else suggests compromises their freedom. And when someone does that in front of other people, there's an overlay of embarrassment to boot.

In the context of a couple's buying decision, however the reality is that the woman's point of view is very much a part of the process. In the presence of a salesperson, this can lead to some complicated interpersonal dynamics.

When buying a car, a computer, or an insurance policy as a part of a couple, some women will jump right in with their own questions and observations; but others simply won't talk much in front of the salesperson, holding their comments until the couple is alone. Then, she can raise her objections and express her preferences much more directly, without her feeling "bossy" or his feeling "henpecked."

From a salesperson's perspective, though, there's a pretty big downside: you don't get the chance to hear her reactions and answer her concerns, which significantly reduces your chances of finalizing the sale. She will share her thoughts with him on the way home, and they may well return the item the next day. Think of the paperwork! Also, and no less important, you will have missed a chance to build rapport with her – and the consequent recommendations and referrals that generates.

So how can you ensure that she surfaces her objections on the spot, where you'll have the opportunity to address them?

One thing you can do is to ask her directly for her questions and reactions. Telling you what she wants in response to your questions is usually a more comfortable dynamic than contradicting and disagreeing with her husband in front of you.

Also, as you're wrapping up the appointment, be sure to excuse yourself for a few moments to give them some privacy as they finalize the decision. If you let the guy shoot from the hip without consulting with her, she may not have gotten what she wants. And if mama ain't happy, ain't nobody happy. Especially you, when the sale falls through.

Service, Support, and Sustaining the Customer Relationship

Reduce the Risk of Buying Your Product

Research shows that women are more interested in, and put more weight on, **warranties, guarantees, and customer support hot lines** – the back end or post-purchase features. As it turns out, women handle the majority of "problem resolution" duties for the household – including handling 65 percent of car repair visits, for example. Consequently, it should be no surprise that women want to be sure that they have help if they encounter problems with the product.

A number of research studies have shown that if a customer has a complaint about your product or service, and the complaint is resolved to her satisfaction, the customer will end up being *more* loyal and more satisfied than a customer who never had a complaint to begin with! Some marketing and sales executives joke that they should build in a little glitch – with a great response plan ready to roll into action, of course – just to increase the overall customer satisfaction level.

Customer Service Is the New Sales

The fact is, there aren't that many companies that truly satisfy customer concerns or complaints. Instead, one often gets stuck in an endless menu on the phone, and when you do reach a voice from the Land of the Living, the answer is ultimately that nothing can be done about your problem anyway.

For anyone reading this who says, "That's not our customer policy," let me say two things. First, of course it's not! No one makes a commitment to delivering bad customer service. Second, try using your own customer service number anonymously – not from a company phone. I'm afraid that you're likely to discover what most customers discover: the service is terrible. That's right; I said it, and I bet you've probably said it, too, about other companies. But most people believe their own press about their company.

I heard of one study that included the question "Would you come back to _____?" in reference to the company that had sold the product. Of the people who answered no, not one mentioned the product; all of them instead identified *a service-related problem.*

If customer service resolves the problem and does so via a caring, intelligent person on the phone who genuinely wants to help reach a resolution, it's surprising and delightful. The companies who actually seem to be getting this, in my experience, are HMOs. For example, I had Aetna as my medical insurance provider, but the sponsoring company recently switched everyone over to United Health Care. Frankly, I dreaded the switch, because Aetna customer service was so good, but to my immense surprise and pleasure, UHC's customer-service people were equally as good.

A customer letter to Geico praising its service and one particular claims adjuster, Mark Newman, recently traveled all the way up the corporate ladder to Tony Nicely, the CEO. (No, I did not make up that name!) What had the adjuster done to deserve it? He'd given his customer his home and cell phone numbers so she could reach him after hours, because it was difficult for her to try to call him during the day.

This one small courtesy made a huge difference to the customer, making it immensely easier for her to fit her car problem into her time parameters. She wrote a thank-you note to the company, Tony Nicely wrote a thank-you note back to her, the account was locked in for life, and the customer is now the company's most enthusiastic source of referrals.

Unfortunately, what usually happens when a customer calls with feedback – and let's face it, particularly complaints – is not delightful, and it certainly doesn't engender loyalty or positive word of mouth. Business relationships can have a great deal of similarity to personal relationships in many ways. Here's what women expect from both.

Recognize me when you see me. One of my pet peeves in dealing with companies is that I have to give them all of my information every time – often before they can even check on whether they can answer my question! Northwestern Health System is different, though. They greet me by name as soon as they pick up the phone; they're efficient and helpful as I'm registering for my appointment; and at the end of the call, they run through a quick confirmation check: "Still live at this address? Want to put it on the same credit card as last time?"

Now, I know this is basically a really fancy caller ID system, but the net effect is to give me the feeling I would get from shopping in the same small town store for years. When I "walk in the door" somebody looks up and says, "Hi, Marti. How you doin' today?" And these days, that's really rare.

In Stephen Covey's book *The 7 Habits of Highly Effective People,* he talks about the concept of an "emotional bank account." The idea is that when you're nice to people, you're depositing equity in your emotional bank account with them, and over time it grows and compounds. This means that when something goes wrong, the customer gives you the benefit of the doubt and tries to work with you.

Is Northwestern Health's caller ID system the reason I go there? No, of course not – it's their convenient locations and integrated records system. But it definitely puts a couple of bucks in their emotional bank account whenever I call, because they make it easier and more pleasant to call them than to call anyone else.

Stay in touch now and then, even if you don't want anything. Every so often I get an email from United Airlines, which I fly frequently, telling me about new developments I need to know about – and not trying to get something from me. For instance, it told me about an impending strike by mechanics that might affect my flight choices. Similarly, a friend who bought a Ford got a follow-up call from the dealership a few weeks after she'd purchased it, just letting her know that Ford was there to answer any questions or problems and asking if she liked the car.

Surprise and Delight

Out of the blue, for absolutely no reason, I got a letter from Jeff Bezos of Amazon.com. (Well, he signed it, didn't he?) The letter included ten one-cent stamps and arrived just after the price of stamps went up a penny. "We can't replace your refrigerator light bulb," the letter read, "and we can't make your tuna salad just the way you like it – but we can save you time." It felt as if Jeff himself had taken a peek into my lifestyle and recognized how very busy I am; when am I going to get to the post office for a book of add-on stamps? Jeff did it for me. Cost: ten cents. Customer delight: priceless. You can bet that beats a coupon for return on investment.

Then there was the "Sweetest Day" surprise I got from Peapod a couple of years ago. For all customers who happened to have scheduled a grocery order delivered that day, Peapod included a bouquet of a dozen lovely red roses. It was *not* an incentive, i.e., a reward I claimed for ordering more or ordering sooner. It was a sweet surprise, totally unexpected and forever remembered.

These customer relationship efforts are the equivalent of a wife or mom tucking a little note into the lunch box – it's the thought that counts, and the unexpectedness is part of the value. To women, who pride themselves on being thoughtful and adding a smile to someone else's day, it's a really nice surprise to have someone think of them that way.

One of the most original "nice surprises" I've heard of comes from a financial advisor at Investors Group, the largest financial services company in Canada. Martin Taylor is among the top five percent of the company's producers, and I have no doubt why.

Whenever he gets a new client or significant new business from an existing client, Taylor sends her a jar of homemade apricot jam. The jar even has a hand-lettered label, personalizing it further. The twist on this that I love the most is that his customers often call up and thank *him* for the thank-you. Again, you can be sure they're telling all of their friends about this – and that's how he keeps getting more and more referrals!

None of these suggestions is a world-shaking game changer. Taken together, though, they can make the difference between a woman walking out your door and a woman sending in her friends.

Marti Barletta

The World's Foremost Authority on Today's Mightiest Market — *Women*

To **The Huffington Post,** she's "the High Priestess of Marketing to Women;" to **TIME magazine,** "the Chief Rabbi of the Sheconomy." Renowned business guru **Tom Peters** calls her "the First Lady of Marketing to Women" and **says "she is one of the best presenters, male or female, I've ever seen."**

Marti Barletta uses her **proprietary GenderGenius™ principles and The Buyer Multiplier™ toolkit to help B2C and B2B clients get more customers, and make more money per customer.** Her first book, *Marketing to Women,* is available in 19 languages. Her latest book, *Marketing to PrimeTime Women,* focuses in on the market's high-spending sweet spot – women in their mid-life *prime* – and shows marketers how to use this under-served segment's growth, size and buying power to turbocharge their business results.

As the go-to authority on marketing and selling to women, Barletta has been quoted on CBS, ABC, MSNBC and NPR, as well as in *The Wall Street Journal, The New York Times, The Economist, USA Today, Inc., Fast Company, TIME, Bloomberg Businessweek,* and many other publications worldwide.

A **popular speaker,** she has enjoyed **rave reviews on every continent** except Antarctica, including **countries as diverse** as Australia, Chile, Denmark, Dubai, Japan, Spain and Sweden. She has spoken for hundreds of companies, conferences and associations; and across dozens of industries, including automotive, banking, consumer products, investment services, retail, travel/tourism and real estate development, to name a few. She is proud that **numerous clients have booked her for return appearances** and **sponsored her for speaking series** to their own customers.

Ms. Barletta's **F500 consulting clients** have included Diageo, Ford, GE Appliances, Logitech, Pfizer, Volvo and others (complete list at www.trendsight.com). She has recently expanded her offerings to make them accessible to **mid-size enterprises** via streamlined consulting practices; and **small businesses** will soon be able to access her ideas through webinars, self-study seminars and group coaching.

Her lively style, command of her subject and passion for her topic create engagement and "Aha!" moments among everyone she works with. **She connects easily with audiences and clients, who enjoy her sense of humor and love her practical tactics** tailored specifically to their business issues and opportunities.

Marti's always up for a new opportunity, so if you'd like to learn how to grow your business by bringing in the world's biggest spenders, **please call her at (847) 964-9960.**

Also by Marti Barletta

Marketing to Women
How to Increase Your Share
of the World's Largest Market

Marketing to PrimeTime Women
How to Attract, Convert, and Keep
Boomer Big Spenders

To inquire about special quantity discounts and order more copies of *Selling to Affluent Women* contact the publisher.

Paramount Market Publishing, Inc.
950 Danby Road STE 136
Ithaca NY 14850
Phone: 607-2775-8100
Fax: 607-275-8101
Toll Free: 888-787-8100
email: editors@paramountbooks.com
www.paramountbooks.com

To contact the author
Marti Barletta
The Trendsight Group
Chicago, IL
Phone: 847-964-9960
email: marti.barletta@trendsight.com